MOM Essentials

10 WORDS SUCCESSFUL MOTHERS LIVE BY
– A BIBLE STUDY –

Kasey Johnson

BEACON HILL PRESS
OF KANSAS CITY

Beacon Hill Press of Kansas City
PO Box 419527
Kansas City, MO 64141
www.BeaconHillBooks.com

ISBN 978-0-8341-3224-5

Printed in the
United States of America

Cover Design: Ryan Deo
Interior Design: Sharon Page

Library of Congress Cataloging-in-Publication Data

Johnson, Kasey, 1976-
Mom essentials : 10 words successful mothers live by : a Bible study / Kasey Johnson.
pages cm
Includes bibliographical references.
ISBN 978-0-8341-3224-5 (pbk.)
1. Mothers—Religious life—Textbooks. 2. Motherhood—Religious aspects—Christianity—Textbooks.
I. Title.
BV4529.18.J635 2014
248.8'431—dc23

2014012204

10 9 8 7 6 5 4 3 2 1

WHAT OTHERS ARE SAYING

"Kasey knows moms, what makes them tick and what helps them in everyday life. *Mom Essentials* addresses the practical needs of moms by pointing them to the truth revealed in Scripture. It not only inspires moms to think through the stumbling blocks to a fulfilling life—it offers the space to work through the details, knowing moms have to capture the moments when they are available. A wise, busy mom herself, Kasey offers a holistic tool that addresses moms' needs from the hands-on to the heart's core."

—Alexandra Kuykendall
Leader and Mom Content Editor, MOPS International
Author, *The Artist's Daughter: A Memoir*

"I really appreciate Kasey's lighthearted, conversational style. . . . It was easy to read and hard to put down! Great words of wisdom and application. . . . I could use this study with fellow believers along with women I want to reach out to."

—Jade V.
Mom to children ages nine and seven

"*Mom Essentials* is like boot camp for harried moms—a basic training to help women in the trenches of life's most demanding job. I've loved learning how to be put together, shaped-up, and equipped to do God's work here and now!"

—Wendy C.
Mom to children ages seven and five

"People think that just because your children are grown you don't feel the same angst as you did when you were a young mom. It's not true. When grandchildren come along and your children face life's battles you are still a mom, and all of us need to remember these essentials and the important role they play in how effective we are as moms, wives, friends, and yes—grandmas!"

—Carolyn
Grandmother to five and mom to two adult children

"I loved looking up the scriptures and writing them down. It helped me engage with the verses and remember the key words and points from each chapter. . . . Kasey uses Scripture and study questions to help lead moms of all ages to a deeper reliance on Jesus and a fuller, more balanced life."

—Amy K.
Mom to children ages seven and five

DEDICATION

This study is dedicated to every mother who longs to not only survive but thrive during the lifelong season of parenting. You are the hands and feet of Jesus, and *you* are making a difference. Thank you for investing in yourself so you can continue to be a blessing to others. You have been made for this time, this place, and for this family—to God be the glory! He is doing great things!

To my husband, Matt, and our amazing children, Matthew, Tyler, and James. Your love and support is more precious than any gift this earth could provide. Thank you for loving me, for being patient, and for believing in the call God has placed in my heart. None of this would matter if you weren't in my life. I love you!

CONTENTS

MOM Essentials

You're getting ready to focus on ten words that are intentionally designed to help you evaluate your life and discover the plan God has for you—no matter your age or the size of your family.

FOREWORD

When I first held my baby boy, Justen, in my arms, I thought about all the things that I wanted to do to raise the best child I could.

I knew I was going to raise a reader, so I read to Justen from the day he was born.

I knew that he would be a man of God, so I took him to church, prayed for him, and raised him on the great heroes of the Bible that I wanted him to emulate.

I knew that he would be athletic, so I bought him his first little A's uniform and pledged to start throwing him a ball as soon as those chubby hands could wrap around it. I had a lot of plans for Justen. But the one thing I forgot to include in my master plan? I forgot about me.

In the midst of trying to be the kind of mom who blended my own homemade baby food and only used cotton diapers on my baby's precious bum, in the midst of attending to every one of my baby's needs (real or perceived), I forgot to take care of his mom. I forgot to include me in the plan.

After a couple of years of living completely for my child, I descended into a dark place. The place of never getting fully dressed (you know that pajamas are perfectly acceptable outerwear as long as you only go to Wal-Mart), reheating instead of cooking, and counting getting up to change the channel (because I long ago lost the remote in some "stash and dash" cleaning spree when my in-laws were coming over) as aerobic exercise.

I forgot about me.

The focus of my parenting—Justen—was all wrong. Because the more lost and miserable I was in my own life, the more it affected how I mothered. Justen wasn't getting the best of me because there was no longer a best of me.

I was filling my days with junk—junk food, junk TV, and junk friends who were more interested in what celebrity kids were doing than their own children. When I finally started to see how far I'd strayed from the kind of mom—the kind of person—I wanted to be, I came to the end of myself. I realized that what goes in (where we spend our limited time and energy) is what will eventually come out of us.

Now, several years later, I've come to understand what it takes to be the kind of mom and person I want to be: intention.

I need to be intentional in every aspect of my life.

I need to be intentional about my time with God.

I need to be intentional about my time with those who build into me, as I build into them.

It's not about being the best at anything. It's about being intentional in the choices we make to lead us to joy and peace.

Make a choice today to intentionally complete this study. The journey will be worth the investment. Invite some of your friends and family to take this journey with you.

You're getting ready to focus on ten words that are intentionally designed to help you evaluate your life and discover the plan God has for you—no matter your age or the size of your family.

A woman who is filled with peace and joy? That's the kind of mom I want raising my child. I pray you'll take time to connect with each chapter, each essential, and rediscover the mom you were meant to be. The mom who loves her kids, but takes time to invest in herself as well. The mom who realizes that God has an amazing plan not only for her kids, but for her as well.

—Kathi Lipp
Author and Speaker

A NOTE FROM KASEY

You are already successful because you are doing what you can, and you are doing it well.

How do you define success?

The American poet and educator Henry Wadsworth Longfellow defined success as "nothing more than doing what you can do, well." We are women. We are mothers. We do many things very well. We are successful because we wake up each day, ready to fulfill our role to the best of our abilities, and we never give up.

Each of us has a success story. A time when all the energy, sleepless nights, planning, and praying came together in a beautiful moment of accomplishment. Moments when mothers say things like:

"No accidents all day, and she went potty three times!"

"He took the trash out without being asked!"

"During her freshman year of college, my daughter called to tell me thank you."

"My daughter asked her friends to stop making fun of another student."

"Our son worked two jobs to raise enough money to attend a mission trip with our church."

Throughout our mothering career, we'll define success differently. However, no matter the age of our children, we are unified in our desire to achieve success according to God's standards. We know he is *for* us (**Romans 8:28**) and by studying Scripture, we discover more about God's plan for our life. The ten essentials we're discovering don't have any merit unless they are grounded in the Word of God.

I understand that completing this study will not guarantee external success. But as we study Scripture, we can enjoy an internal transformation that's sure to bring a new purpose and perspective to our role as mother.

You are already successful because you are doing what you can, and you are doing it well. I pray that through the power of the Holy Spirit at work in your life, you will finish this study feeling encouraged, challenged, and empowered to be exactly the kind of mom God has called you to be.

Since becoming a mom, God has been putting me together in new ways and challenging me. He's been shaping my heart to hear his voice and respond. Writing this study has reminded me how ill-equipped I am when I try to do something in my own strength. I need God with me at all times in order for anything I attempt to be considered "successful."

Right now, this moment can become a success story for you. This can be a time when you truly begin to trust in the Lord, to delight in him and commit your ways to him (**Psalm 37**). Thank you for cherishing your role as a mother and for taking time to know more about the Creator who called you to this wonderful but sometimes overwhelming task of raising the next generation.

You are my sister in Christ, and I can't wait to see how God moves in our lives and in turn in the lives of our children. We can go into the world with confidence, as Scripture shows us what it truly means to be successful.

—Kasey

1

MOM MOMENT

Hebrews 4:12: "For the word of God is alive and active. Sharper than any double-edged sword, it penetrates even to dividing soul and spirit, joints and marrow; it judges the thoughts and attitudes of the heart."

THE ESSENTIALS

Mom Essential: BALANCE

Some of my favorite childhood memories involve watching the Olympics with my mother. We both loved gymnastics and the amazing athletes who executed difficult routines with incredible grace and strength. The balance beam routines always made me nervous. Seeing an athlete hover four feet above the ground on a four-inch beam seemed a bit too risky for me. Did you know only women compete on the beam? I learned this fact when I heard a commentator talking with one of the young ladies who was competing. As the interview continued, the athlete was asked how she completed her aerial elements and poses. She said the secret to being successful was to know where the beam was at all times. Even when she wasn't able to look down, she could feel it under her feet. While turning in the air, her eyes would search for the beam and allow her to return to its solid surface.

Along with athletic competition, our family enjoys watching television shows that portray people accomplishing amazing physical feats. Thousands were glued to their television in 2013 as Nik Wallenda walked a quarter of a mile over a Grand Canyon gorge on a tightrope. Throughout the event, television correspondents kept their viewers informed. They focused on the width of the rope, the distance below Nik's feet, and the fact that no safety harnesses or ropes were being used. In his hands, Nik held a long balance pole that ran parallel to the ground. Thanks to a microphone clipped to his shirt, we could hear every word Nik uttered as he made the almost thirty-minute journey from one rock formation to the next. I was pleasantly surprised as I heard him speak prayers to God. Wallenda asked God to help him focus, to bring him peace, and at one point he asked God to help the cable stop swaying so much in the wind.

As women, we are usually very good at keeping our lives balanced and focused. It's when unplanned or new situations occur that our confidence can begin to waver a bit. We might not be standing on a four-inch beam or hovering above the Grand Canyon, but finding a balance between who we are, what we do, and what we are becoming can feel like an equally daunting task.

WHO WE ARE

As we begin our time of study, we first need to know who we are as women of God. "Put Together" is our theme for chapters 2, 3, and 4. Just as a builder lays a solid foundation before construction continues, so we must allow God to put us together at a basic level. Every thought, source of strength, and possible hidden issue must come under the watchful eye of the Master Builder—God. Being honest about our lives allows us to accept the peace God offers. When we allow our lives to be put together according to God's plan, we gain an opportunity to discover an end product we never thought possible. The three essentials within these chapters are strength, honesty, and identity.

WHAT WE DO

Discovering who we are helps us cope with the many tasks we complete. As mothers, we are continually growing and changing. Our ability to adapt and grow allows us to meet our family's ever-changing needs. Through our daily tasks and activities we can realize the refining process God initiates in all of our lives. God's plan for our lives becomes a reality when we recognize how God is using his hands to gently, but firmly, shape us. Chapters 5, 6, and 7 have the theme of "Shaped Up." We'll see how what we do helps us discover the essentials of growth, perspective, and discipline. These might sound like heavy topics, but we understand that being in shape physically, financially, and spiritually allows us to effectively manage the rough and sometimes unknown road awaiting us on this parenting journey.

WHAT WE ARE BECOMING

It can feel as though our world revolves around our children, but what happens when our children don't need us anymore or we don't know how to meet their needs? During this time of caring for our family, we need to remember we are investing in something bigger than ourselves and God is working everything together to help us enjoy this season while preparing for seasons to come. During chapters 8, 9, and 10 we'll work through the theme "Equipped." Everyone wants to feel successful at his or her job. Our ability to feel successful depends on the three essentials laid out in these chapters: preparation, networking, and surrender. When we surround ourselves with a support group, have a plan written down, and surrender our lives to the One who made us, we're able to discover a clear purpose and plan for our lives.

Our three themes (put together, shaped up, and equipped) come from combining the New International Version (NIV) and *The Message* (TM) translations of **2 Timothy 3:16-17**. Using an NIV Bible, fill in the words that are missing from Paul's second letter to Timothy in chapter 3, verses 16 through 17:

"All ______________________ is God-breathed and is useful

for ______________________, rebuking, correcting and training

in righteousness, so that the servant of God may be thoroughly

______________________ for every good work."

Eugene Peterson restates Paul's words to Timothy in *The Message* (a paraphrase of Scripture that utilizes our current vocabulary) by writing: "Every part of Scripture is God-breathed and useful one way or another—showing us truth, exposing our rebellion, correcting our mistakes, training us to live God's way. Through the Word we are put together and shaped up for the tasks God has for us."

Paul's words are powerful and straight to the point. I don't necessarily see myself as being rebellious or needing to be rebuked, but I am certain to make mistakes, and I know I need more training. God has given us an incredible task—we're moms. We are balancing a million different thoughts, needs, events, and emotions all at the same time. I wish I could sit down with you at a coffee shop and honestly ask, "How are you doing?" My hope would be an honest answer in return and that both of us would finish our time feeling encouraged, focused, and energized. Since we can't meet for coffee, I've been praying over the words and pages of this study. My prayer is that through God's divine intercession, our time together would be like a burst of adrenaline and joy to your spirit. I pray you'll enjoy each moment as God puts you together, shapes you up, and equips you to be the woman and mother your family needs.

No matter the ages of our children, we will always be moms, and to some of us that sounds a bit exhausting. Whether our children are grown or just learning to crawl, we are members of the same team. We're on the front lines and in the trenches. As mothers, we are getting the job done.

The beautiful part about a community filled with mothers is that each of us brings different perspectives, experiences, gifts, and issues to the group. No one wants to be the weak link, but let's face it—each of us knows what it feels like to mourn the loss of sleep, our figure, our memory, and even control over our lives.

The sacrifices that come with accepting the title of "mom" can seem overwhelming, unless we find a source that will help us find a balance and keep us focused on what matters most.

So, how are you doing? What season of life are you experiencing right now? Take a moment to record today's date and your current struggles, joys, and situation:

Today's Date: ____________________

____

____

When we write things down, we keep our memory and perspective in check. It's easy to forget how tough or wonderful things were in our past because our present situation can become overwhelming. For most of us, we will be dealing with new issues or perhaps will have found resolution to others by the time we finish this study. My prayer is that each of us can look back and see God's faithfulness within each essential and theme we encounter together.

Throughout life we will face a constantly changing landscape of issues, decisions, and challenges. What's a mom to do when each day brings an element of the unknown? Hold tightly to what is known!

We can say with confidence, and know for certain, that Scripture and prayer can make a difference in our lives and bring balance when we feel shaken. In Matthew

24:35, Jesus declares how certain his words (or Scripture) are. Using your Bible, read the verse from Matthew and fill in the missing words:

> "Heaven and earth will ____________ _____________, but my words will _________________ pass away."

The season we are currently experiencing will pass because in this life, change is a certainty. In spite of the changes around us, it is wonderful to know we have something as timeless as the Bible. We can cling to Scripture when nothing on earth makes sense. As we navigate the pages of this study together, I am certain we are making a forever impact on our personal growth and spiritual health. When we are grounded in something as perfect as Scripture, we will be able to care for our family and enjoy our role as mothers no matter what challenges come our way.

When my boys were young, I felt like I was managing a three-ring circus more than running a home. One day, I was hoping to find some quiet time with God while the boys took a nap. Sitting at our kitchen table, I opened my journal and Bible, ready to dive into God's Word. I couldn't have been more than four words into my reading when I promptly fell asleep. Thirty minutes later, I awoke to find a drool stain on my journal and my pen still resting in my hand. I was a bit embarrassed and started to apologize to the Lord when a familiar scripture came to my mind. I remembered hearing it on the Christian radio station, and the words quieted my mind as I allowed the truth of Scripture to invade my heart. Discover this gracious invitation from Jesus in **Matthew 11:28**:

> "Come to me, all you who are ________________ and _____________________, and I will give you _____________."

Immediately I stopped feeling guilty about my impromptu nap. Instead, I smiled and thanked God for the much-needed rest. I have to wonder if he smiled too. Clearly, I needed some physical rest in order to make it through the afternoon and evening. The beautiful finish to that particular day came when later that night I was able to study my Bible and listen to God's voice without exhaustion creeping in.

Some of us need physical renewal while others are longing for a renewed connection with the Lord. Think back to your upbringing and exposure to Scripture. Are you comfortable reading Scripture, or does it seem a bit overwhelming to you? Have you connected with a particular Bible verse in the past? Would you be able to explain the basic components of the Bible and its content?

"I no longer call you servants, because a servant does not know his master's business. Instead, I have called you friends, for everything that I learned from my Father I have made known to you."

—John 15:15

These questions help us know where we are in our walk with the Lord and what we need in order to achieve a balanced and productive spiritual life. If you have questions about the Bible, I encourage you to reach out to other women in your church or to a pastor from your local church. When you know what you are studying and how it is constructed, you'll benefit even more from the time you are investing.

I believe God speaks to us in unique and powerful ways, though the ability to listen and respond to God's voice can be challenging. One of the essential elements to living a balanced life comes when we place a high priority on reading, understanding, and applying Scripture.

Reading Scripture is essential. The truths we discover in the Bible help form our perspective on life, how we apply our faith, and how we respond to situations. When the enemy (Satan) comes against us with feelings of fear, inadequacy, or despair, we can turn to the Bible. Within its pages we discover people just like us. We learn the details behind their struggles, and we see how God's hand moved in their lives. The application of this knowledge comes when we reflect on how God might be moving in our lives and using the situations around us to help us grow.

John 15:15 says that Jesus has revealed everything he has learned from his Father. Isn't that beautiful? When we are folding laundry, making meals, and carpooling, we aren't alone. God is with us each moment. And whether

Because we have a relationship with God and understand that he is love, we also know that God's actions come from his desire to invest in our lives.
#MomEssentials

we realize it or not, his master plan is becoming a reality through our daily actions. Only the Creator of the heavens and the earth could infuse such a beautiful truth into seemingly mundane events. God has given us every tool we need to be successful; it's up to us to discover and apply each one. Through reading Scripture, God shows us what should be essential in our lives and, in turn, we discover a new sense of balance.

Looking back to our Mom Moment for this chapter, write in your own words what **Hebrews 4:12** tells us about the words in the Bible:

When we read Scripture, we can have confidence that it is more than just stories or sayings. It is an active, living presence in our lives and although the thought of being judged might not sound appealing to some, we know we serve a God of mercy and grace.

Understanding what we read in Scripture comes from having a relationship with God. This relationship is established and strengthened through an active prayer life.

Prayer is essential. I believe the words from Hebrews 4 are true. Scripture is living and active in the physical and spiritual world. The promises found in the Bible will become a reality in our lives through the essential activity of prayer. Having constant conversations with God trains us to seek him first and teaches us how to hear his voice. The best part about prayer is that it can occur anywhere and anytime. Can you think of a time when you were praying and no one around you knew you were talking with the

Creator of the universe? Have you experienced unplanned moments of quiet connection with God? Whether we offer praises or requests to God, prayer is essential for strengthening our relationship with him and maintaining balance in our lives.

According to Hebrews 4 the word of God can judge "the thoughts and attitudes of the heart" (**Hebrews 4:12*b***). When I read Scripture, my heart and mind become cleansed and challenged. I love that Scripture can be read again and again by different people, all the while providing fresh revelations and insight. Sometimes we discover scriptures that pierce us to the core. When this happens we recognize the living, active presence of the Holy Spirit as he uses the words we are studying to help us become stronger and wiser. Our response to this growth is to pray. Through prayer we learn more about the God who created us and loves us.

One of my favorite devotional books is Oswald Chambers' *My Utmost for His Highest*. Chambers writes about the topic of prayer, and I tend to think God laid this on Chambers' heart specifically for people like me. Chambers writes,

"To say that 'prayer changes things' is not as close to the truth as saying, 'Prayer changes me and then I change things'. . . . Prayer is not a matter of changing things externally, but one of working miracles in a person's inner nature."[1]

When disaster strikes, prayer is typically our first response and that is fine, because God is listening and answering those prayers. However, if we want to live a truly balanced life, we need to be intentional about making prayer a priority at all times so it can change us from the inside. Read **Ephesians 6:18** and fill in the missing words from this powerful scripture:

"And pray in the Spirit on __________ ____________________
with all kinds of _________________ and requests. With this in
mind, be alert and _______________ keep on __________________
for all the Lord's people."

Whether life is good or bad, during all occasions, we should pray. Even when we don't understand what is happening and our situation makes it difficult to put our thoughts into sentences, we can still pray. Chambers was right—prayer is meant as an internal vehicle for growth and change, more than a cure for our external circumstances. That's why prayer is such an essential part of our spiritual life and growth.

We understand that prayer and Scripture reading should be considered essential, but how can we be expected to fit these into our already busy lives? One way to help find time is to separate the essentials in our lives from the extras. Some of the extras that come to my mind include pedicures, specialty coffee, and even chocolate. (I know. I gasp to even type such a phrase!) Staying focused on the essentials in our lives becomes more challenging as the demands on our time and energy increase. Our physical well-being depends on some very important essentials like shelter, air, water, food, and sleep. These items are essential because without them, we could not go on living. When it comes to our spiritual life and health, we need to recognize how essential prayer and Scripture should be. They make the difference between our spiritual life thriving or dying, just as food, water, or air.

Balance is our essential for this chapter, and sometimes it can feel as though we're standing on a tightrope or four-inch beam trying desperately to strike a balance between the extras and essentials in our lives. Take a moment to define the essentials in your life (these are outside of shelter, air, water, food, and sleep). These items will be different for everyone. It's important to remember we are functioning within a "no judgment zone." The essentials we're looking for are anything that, when present, help your life feel fulfilled and complete. Take a moment and write down some of the items you view as essentials in your life:

____

____

____

____

Using the essentials from your list as a starting point, we're going to fill in a chart called "The Essentials in My Life." After listing your essentials in the first column, record how much time per week it requires. For example, if one of your essentials is to exercise, record the average amount of time needed each week in order for this essential to be effective and completed. The last column is provided so you can categorize each essential as meeting a physical, emotional, or spiritual need. Some essentials might fulfill all three; you be the judge concerning how the item(s) impact your world. My personal chart is provided as an example and starting place, but I would encourage you to create yours first before referencing the example I've provided.

THE ESSENTIALS IN MY LIFE

Essential	Average Hours Weekly	Area

THE ESSENTIALS IN MY LIFE (KASEY'S CHART)

Essential	Average Hours Weekly	Area
Alone time with Matt	26	emotional
Exercise	4	physical, emotional
Work (time with other adults)	40	emotional
Writing (personal reflection)	5	spiritual, emotional
Talking to my mom on the phone	8	emotional
Time with friends	2	all three
Church worship services	3	emotional, spiritual

I have to be honest: the first chart I filled out looked a bit different from this final version. I began writing things down, and after looking at my list, I discovered some "extras" snuck in, disguised as essentials. So I asked myself this question: "If the particular item/activity didn't occur during my week, what sort of impact would that have on my well-being and life?" Take a look at your chart and apply the answer to this question for each of your essentials. Do they still work, or should they move to the "extras"? Finding a balance between the two groups can be tough—thank you for being transparent and open to God's leading.

When we truly allow God to put us together in a new way, to reshape our perspective and equip us with the tools we need to be successful, we'll be able to balance the essentials and extras in our lives. Notice I used the word "allow" in this sentence. We serve a God that is persistent but never pushy. He is faithful, never fickle. As human beings we tend to take on the traits of pushy and fickle, so we need to decide here and now if we will truly allow God room to move in our lives. When I'm tempted to think God needs my help I remember the Lord's words from **Isaiah 55:8**:

"'For my ________________ are not your thoughts, neither are your __________ my ways,' declares the LORD."

I hope my thoughts and my ways continue to become more like God's, but for now I'm so thrilled that God accepts me just as I am and promises to make me more than I ever dreamed I could be. I love the idea of being put together, shaped up, and equipped to fulfill my calling as a mom. Although this sounds like a monumental task, we serve a mighty God. No matter our background or upbringing, God is ready to do a beautiful work and bring balance into our lives.

As we close out our first chapter together, I'd like to ask you to read aloud the commitment below and sign your name. This is a promise to be persistent, not perfect. How much and how quickly you cover the content is not the goal. Instead, I pray you'll discover how truly beautiful, unique, and amazing you are. God has wonderful things in store for us. I can't wait to discover them with you!

"I, ______________________________________,
choose to commit myself to the study of Scripture and the practice of an active prayer life. I want God to put me together, shape me, and equip me in order that I might fulfill my role as a child of God and as a mother."

Signed: ______________________________

Today's Date: ___________________________

CLOSING PRAYER

God, there are days when I feel as though I'm walking on a tightrope while trying to balance everything and everyone in my life. I know I'm blessed to carry the title "mother," but sometimes I wish I could cry out for help and admit that I don't have all the answers. I know you hear my cries, and I praise you for being a God that cares about my every need and the needs of my family. Help me get rid of any extras taking up my time and focus on the essentials. I commit my life to you. Help me to see my life in a fresh way and enjoy a renewed sense of balance. I love you, Lord. Amen.

THEME 1

PUT TOGETHER

2

STRENGTH SOURCE

Mom Essential:
STRENGTH

MOM MOMENT

Psalm 105:4: "Look to the LORD and his strength; seek his face always."

I was in the sixth grade and excited to be with my friends from school on our field trip. My parents had given me a little money to spend in the gift shop and I was proud of my purchase: a set of bookmarks. As I recounted our trip for my parents, I proudly read the sayings and quotes from my bookmarks. One of them said, "If it is to be, it is up to me." Initially I read that phrase and thought the quote showed confidence while echoing my desire to accept any challenge that came my way.

The look on my parents' faces quickly alerted me to the fact that they did not interpret the saying in the same way. I asked what was wrong, and they lovingly educated me concerning the origin and meaning behind such a statement. In my youth, I didn't know that by speaking this phrase I was saying I could do everything and anything all on my own. Basically, I was boasting in my own strength and unknowingly saying I didn't need anyone or any help.

As a grown woman, I've learned to appreciate my strengths and my weaknesses, even though I don't enjoy admitting there are areas of life where I struggle. I used to see weakness as a negative trait. After many attempts to be everything to everyone, I call my weaknesses by a different name—I call them limitations. Perhaps it's a bit of a mind game, but for whatever reason, I'm able to accept the term "limitations" much easier than I can accept the word "weakness." I now understand that relying on my own strength for all areas of life would leave me feeling very lonely, overwhelmed, and stressed. Being a mom is tough; trying to do it alone can be detrimental.

When it comes to fulfilling every responsibility and completing each task in our day, our strength can quickly be depleted. The world offers various sources we can use to replenish our strength. As Christians we understand these sources to be short-lived and sometimes inadequate, but many women reach for these options when things get tough. In your opinion, circle the most prominent strength sources people gravitate toward when their weaknesses (or limitations) become a reality:

EDUCATION	ACCOMPLISHMENTS
FAMILY BACKGROUND	BUSY SCHEDULE
JOB TITLE	IQ
MONEY/SHOPPING	SOCIAL STATUS
PHYSICAL STATURE	SUBSTANCES

Each of these sources can initially appear as positive and healthy, but even good intentions can develop negative results. When the world's strength sources (like the ones we circled) become idols in our lives, or become our primary strength source, we forget to seek God's face.

Have you endured some particularly tough events in the past? What were some of your strength sources during the tough times? There are no wrong answers. Just be honest and write down who or what helped you make it through:

During my biggest struggles in life, God has been faithful to provide peace and strength through Scripture. In chapter 1, we established that, in our lives, reading Scripture shouldn't be seen as an extra, but as an essential. Many times a verse from the Bible or a sentence from a devotional reading can bring the peace, strength, direction, and even the rebuke we need. Sometimes I handle the tough times with uncharacteristic grace and strength. During other moments I struggle to put on a happy face and make it through the day.

Thinking back to our worldly sources of strength, it's easy to see how quickly we can begin to rely on any one of those items. After all, they are easily accessible and yet incredibly counterfeit. When the world's strength runs out and we still have a battle to fight, we can rely on a never-ending, powerful strength source: Sovereign God. Take a moment to look back to the beginning of this chapter and read our mom essential from **Psalm 105:4**.

David, the writer of many psalms, knew what it meant to struggle and have his emotional, spiritual, and physical strength completely depleted. Throughout the Psalms we read David's songs and prayers to God. Some verses are filled with praise, others with pleading, and still other verses reveal that King David questioned God. Wow! David was completely real and transparent with God. In return, David was able to see the true strength and power God provides to those who need him. In verse 4, what are we told to do? Fill in the missing words to discover how we can discover our strong, powerful, and capable God.

"_____________ to the LORD and his strength; _____________ his face always" (Psalm 105:4).

As women and mothers, I think it takes a lot to truly find the end of our strength. My friends and I joke about it, but for many of us the following scenario is all too true: we could have a fever and be throwing up and still find a way to get laundry done, feed our children, care for them, and even make dinner. We don't know the meaning of the word "can't," mostly because for many of us we don't have a choice—we have to keep going! Even though we are incredibly capable, we are still human and our humanity brings limitations. We must choose to look at and seek after the Lord. Our focus needs to remain on God and not on our situation.

Because God is divine, he isn't bound by physical limitations. Throughout Scripture we discover how strong God is. Because of our relationship with Christ, we can claim his strength as our own. Let's discover some of the scriptures that describe how God's strength helps us when we seek him during difficult times. Fill in the missing words as you read through these essential scriptures.

- **Deuteronomy 31:6**: "Be strong and courageous. Do not be afraid or terrified because of them, for the LORD your God __________ __________ ________; he will never leave you nor forsake you."
- **2 Chronicles 15:7**: "But as for you, ______ ____________ and do not give up, for your work will be ___________________."
- **Isaiah 41:10**: "________ _______ _________ __________, for I am with you; do not be dismayed, for I am your God. I will ____________________ you and help you; I will ____________ you with my righteous right ____________."
- **1 Thessalonians 3:13*a***: "May he _______________________ __________ _______________ so that you will be blameless and holy in the presence of our God."

Each of these verses contains a form of the verb "be." These "be verbs" describe an action we are to live out during tough times. Reread our four scriptures and draw a bracket ([]) around the "be" phrase that we, as followers of Christ, are responsible for carrying out.

After you place a bracket around the "be" phrases that describe what our reactions should be, go back through the same verses and draw a circle around the words in each scripture that define what God will do.

Using your markings, fill in the chart by writing the Scripture reference in the first column, our response ("be" phrase in brackets) in the second column, and God's response (words that are circled) in the third column. Deuteronomy is done for you as an example:

Scripture	Our Response	God's Response
Deuteronomy 31:6	Be strong and courageous.	He goes with you.

These scriptures provide a beautiful picture of God's constant and complete strength. He is God; he doesn't need anything, yet Scripture tells us that God's strength is made perfect in our weakness. When God is our strength, we can stand strong no matter what, or who, comes against us! (See **Philippians 4:13**.)

Suffering is an all too common theme involved in living on earth. Some people who suffer the most are the ones trying to do the most good for our world. The apostle Paul was one of these people. Before Paul met God, his name was Saul. Saul hated Christians and even persecuted those who declared their love for Jesus Christ. Amidst all this hate, God still loved Saul and sought him out. When Saul met God on a dirt road (read all about it in Acts 9), his life and his name were forever changed. Saul became Paul and his life was sold out to God. He was determined to share God's love with everyone.

As a messenger of God, Paul was given the incredible responsibility to help the early church understand what it meant to be a Christian. As he traveled and spoke, he was tempted to find strength through accolades and acknowledgment. God put a "thorn in [his] flesh" to keep him humble. In 2 Corinthians Paul asked three times for this thorn to be removed. We don't know exactly what that thorn was, but we do know the Lord's response. Take a moment to read **2 Corinthians 12:9-10** and fill in the blanks below.

"But he said to me, 'My grace is

____________________________ ___________

__________, for my power is made

perfect in __________________________."

Therefore I will boast all the more gladly

about my ____________________________,

so that Christ's ____________________

may rest on me. That is why, for

Christ's sake, I ____________________ in

______________________, in insults, in

_____________________, in persecutions, in

difficulties. For when I am __________, then

I am strong.'"

I can do all this through him who gives me strength.
—Philippians 4:13

A part of me wishes Paul's prayer for God to take away whatever was causing him pain were different. Knowing Paul was suffering, God would have said, "Sure thing—consider it gone." But then I remember the rest of this verse. If Paul never suffered, if he never had to deal with the tough things in this life, he wouldn't have needed God's strength. Our Creator knows us better than we know ourselves, and while I don't believe God puts bad things in our lives just to keep us dependent upon him, I do believe God wants us to discover why a relationship with him is so essential, especially because we live in a sinful world.

Sin is all around us, and our weaknesses will be tested and tried more than we'd like. Do you have a "thorn in your flesh"? Perhaps it's a co-worker, boss, child's personality, or housing situation—whatever it might be, we have to acknowledge the real possibility that God has allowed that "thorn" to remain in order for our weakness to show God's power being made perfect in us. Giving only as much detail as you feel comfortable, use the space provided to describe the current issue(s) that brings stress and anxiety into your life. What's your "thorn"?

____

____

Look back at **2 Corinthians 12:9-10**. How do these words apply to your situation? How are God's grace and strength being worked out and seen? Are you able to delight in spite of your circumstance and give God the glory for what he is doing in your life?

____

____

Sometimes it feels like the title of "mom" brings a kind of superpower with it. We begin living for others and we will do whatever it takes to make sure the people we love are cared for. When life gets tough; when husbands leave; when jobs are lost; when children are taken to heaven too early, that's when our superpower meets its nemesis. During these difficult times, Satan can try to lie to us and say that God has left us or is against us. But Paul tells us that God's grace is sufficient and his power is even stronger when we feel weak.

The statements we've read are truth. However, it's important to take a moment and recognize there will be times when we are so exhausted or overwhelmed that weakness will feel as though it's winning. These are the times when we have no more tears to cry or words to say. In these moments our pain is real, but our weakness isn't stronger than our Savior's promise to strengthen and uphold us (see chart on page 30). When life begins to fall apart, we can surrender ourselves to our God and allow him to put us back together piece by piece.

Our family, friends, and even our fellow church members can help in this process, but we have to be willing to admit that even our mommy superpower isn't enough. We need God's strength.

During the spring of 2010 I discovered what it felt like to be completely broken, empty, and unable to do things on my own. One morning my eye stopped closing when I blinked. I would try to drink from a cup and the liquid would simply roll out the corner of my mouth and onto my chin. The diagnosis of Bell's palsy came as a shock, and the months that followed were filled with tears, medication, pain, and research. My mother flew in from California to take care of the boys, and thanks to her quick response I was able to rest and heal. No amount of positive thinking, striving, or effort was going to change my reality—only God's strength would suffice.

As a mother to three boys I try to emphasize table manners and good eating habits, but the left side of my mouth wouldn't respond so I had to get creative. In order to eat I had to take tiny bites, tilt my head so it touched my right shoulder, and hold a napkin over my lips on my left side. Talk about humbling! The worst part was the issue of my left eyelid never closing. My eye was the most painful part of the whole thing, and I found myself taping my eye shut and wearing a patch almost twenty-four hours a day.

We tried to find humor in the situation. Whether we were practicing pirate-speak or the boys were asking me to drink out of a cup so they could watch the liquid dribble down my chin, there were definitely times when laughter was the best medicine. The boys learned to stay away from my left side and kissing them on the cheek became awkward. . . . those were the moments when I really missed what my face used to do.

This condition has changed me forever. I now have a built-in "shut off" button. I used to be able to manage a million things at once, but not anymore. When I start to think through my to-do list I can feel my cheek starting to droop. I have to take a deep breath and refuse to let the anxiety overtake me.

My brother says I don't know when to stop, so God put a little switch in me to help me learn when to take a break

When life begins to fall apart, we can surrender ourselves to our God and allow him to put us back together piece by piece.
#MomEssentials

NOTES

and slow down. I think he's right. As moms, we accept our reality as it comes our way. Sometimes we deal with each child, each situation, and each day without stopping to evaluate the effect they can have on us.

Before this happened, I didn't know what "stressed out" felt like because I lived there all the time. I thought I was good at juggling things, and some would say I was. I could keep my cool, answer questions, and keep a smile on my face, but let's be honest—all those cheery, well-balanced public moments are draining. I don't think I realized how to listen to my body when it was telling me to slow down. Mostly I didn't think I gave myself the chance to listen to such a request.

Well, I don't have the luxury of not listening anymore. This is it. My face is going to fall off (well, at least fall down) if I don't slow down! So I've learned a new way of life. I've found a new freedom in discovering that I do have limitations, I do need rest, and I do deserve a break.

So here's my challenge for all of us: at least twice a day we need to stop, sit down, put our feet up, take five slow deep breaths, and relax. The simple act of breathing slowly and putting my feet up for a couple of minutes makes a world of difference when it comes to dealing with everything the day throws at me.

You may not have half of your face falling off, but I hope my experience can act as a warning bell to all moms—*know your limits*, listen to your body, and please don't apologize for taking a moment to refuel!

I took time to reevaluate and tweak my life, but I would have *never* made it through this time without my friends. They helped save my face too! Women from our Sunday school class brought meals, took my boys to playgroup, and offered to clean my house and do the laundry so that I could rest. Sure it was embarrassing to have to wipe the drool from my mouth and talk with only half my lips, but nothing prepared me for how grateful and humbled I felt when friends started coming to my rescue. They were strong when I was weak. It's difficult for me to accept help, but this time I didn't have a choice.

I praise God every day for these women, and I hope one day I'll be able to return the favor in their time of need. This experience taught me to set limits, and I've learned how to ask for help. All of us come to a place when we can no longer manage on our own. It's a crazy place of humility, honesty, and a dose of reality. Remember to rest, renew, and relax this week—take a deep breath. God is our source of strength, an ever-present help in times of trouble (Psalm 46), and he knows exactly what we need and when we need it.

I pray you have a group of women available to help renew your strength and be strong for you when life gets to be too much. My diagnosis has changed me, and I'm still dealing with the physical effects that accompany this condition. The issue isn't going away, but my response to it is finally starting to resemble more of Paul's approach. I remind myself that even when I'm weak, my God is strong and therefore so am I.

Take a moment to claim God's strength for yourself. Let it become a reality and an attainable strength source. Illness, bills piling up faster than your income, loneliness, a child's disabilities—the list of issues, or thorns, can go on and on, but the items on our list will lose their power over us when we claim the promises from the chart we created about God's strength and our responses.

Referencing our chart of four scriptures, I've started four phrases and I would like you to finish them. Complete each statement with something from your own life that needs God's strength infused into it. Perhaps you are already sensing his presence in your situation. If that's the case, to God be the glory! If you'd like to write your own statements, please feel free to do so. The prompts I've provided are simply a starting place and aren't meant to stifle or inhibit your thoughts and experiences.

I need God to go with me as I ______________________________.

I need God to uphold me when ______________________________.

I need God's strength to ______________________________.

I sense God's reward even now when ______________________________.

We'll be tempted to rely on our own strength, but we have to make a conscious choice to rely on God and allow his strength to shine through our weakness. We've spent time discovering some of the scriptures describing God's strength and its availability to us. To review, see if you can remember one of the verses we looked at, **Isaiah 41:10**, and fill in the missing words below.

> "So do not fear, for I am ____________ ____________; do not be dismayed, for I am your God; I will ____________________ you and help you; I will uphold you with my righteous right hand."

Wouldn't it be wonderful to hear moms quote this verse to each other? All of us have either lived through or will someday experience really tough times. I pray we can say with confidence that God held us in his hand. When our strength was gone, he was with us, helping us as we relied on his strength and not our own.

I would love to report that the bookmark I brought home after our field trip was the only time I believed the world's lie that I could do things on my own and in my own strength. If I'm being honest, it was not and probably won't be the last time a selfish ambition will find its way into my spirit, but I'm working hard to identify and limit those occasions. When I'm tempted to rely on my own strength, I remind myself how strong and capable God is.

CLOSING PRAYER

Thank you, God, for being strong enough to help me every day. Please open my eyes to the true strength sources you've provided in my life. Right now I claim your strength for myself. I will lean on you and go with confidence knowing you are with me. I know I can make it through today and tomorrow because you are with me. Help me to glorify you in the small and big moments so that others can discover your strength at work in my life. Lord, help my children see how you are helping me so they too may draw on your strength when they grow tired and weary. I know you are doing amazing things through me each day, and I give you the glory for helping me accomplish so much when I feel like I have so little to give. I pray for my community of moms, that we will feel your strength and in turn be strong for each other. Lord, let others see your strength through my weakness and help me to feel your strength in every situation I face. Amen.

3

CLEANUP ON AISLE "ME"

Mom Essential: HONESTY

MOM MOMENT

Matthew 6:20-21: "But store up for yourselves treasures in heaven, where moths and vermin do not destroy, and where thieves do not break in and steal. For where your treasure is, there your heart will be also."

When someone begins a statement with the words, "Be honest," I start to panic. I wonder if the person really wants me to be honest or if that's my cue to sugarcoat my response. There've been times when I was truly honest, and the result was not positive. Honesty can invite growth or a grudge; it's a tricky essential to apply to our lives and our relationships.

Let's be honest with ourselves. As we look at our Mom Moment for this chapter, we could turn the final sentence into a question. Where is your heart, and what do you treasure? The chart you filled out in chapter 1 helped separate the essentials from the extras in your life. While we strive to keep the essentials high on our priority list, it's very easy for the extras to take up most of our time and become something we unintentionally "treasure." Has anyone asked you the cliché question, "If your house were on fire, what three items would you bring with you before escaping the flames"?

I've encountered that question in various forms while interviewing for jobs and leadership programs, but one day this phrase became a reality. Our children were six, five, and three years old. I picked up pizza on my way home from work. Between traffic and delays at daycare, the pizza had grown cold. I turned on the oven, placed the pizza box on the top shelf, and started making a salad. The boys were playing in the living room when my oldest calmly said, "Mommy, I smell smoke." I smelled it too, and that's when I remembered the pizza. Upon opening the oven door, smoke filled the kitchen, and I saw flames jumping to life with the fresh burst of oxygen I'd provided.

I closed the door, turned off the oven, and told the boys to stay back. I ran to the garage, grabbed the fire extinguisher off the wall, and then realized I didn't know how to use it! By the time I finished reading the instructions, the flames had basically put themselves out. I was a little embarrassed, but glad the immediate danger had passed. Smoke was still pouring out of the oven, the fire alarm began to sound, and I started opening windows. As I opened the back door, I was surprised to see our three boys huddled together on the deck. Our middle son brought humor to the situation when he asked, "Why did you fire the pizza?" I started to usher them back inside when I noticed our oldest son, Matthew, was holding a large book in his hands. I asked if they were okay and Matthew said, "Don't worry, Mom—I brought the boys and your marriage pictures out here so they'd be safe."

I couldn't hold back the tears. I knew I was looking at three of the most important people in my life, but I had no idea my son would choose his three items: his two brothers and our wedding pictures. I don't know exactly what made him think of our wedding album, but it was obvious we had described the pictures inside as being something we treasured. Matthew is currently eleven years old. I would love to think he'd help his brothers outside and again take our wedding album with him, but our essential for this chapter is honesty. So if I'm being honest, he would most likely grab whatever technical/gaming device is closest to him and his football gear. A preteen boy has his priorities, and priorities matter. In order to discover what matters most to us (outside of our family), we have to get down and dirty, and, well, honest.

Every woman, at some point in her life, deals with insecurities, fears, and personal junk. These things start to cloud our understanding of what we treasure and where that treasure lies. The book of Galatians calls this kind of junk "burdens." Some burdens are clearly seen while others can pile up little by little, and one day we're surprised to discover their true weight and magnitude. When we make the unknown known, we find out what burdens we are carrying and how they impact our lives.

David prayed a very honest request in **Psalm 139**. Fill in the missing words from David's prayer found in verses 23 and 24.

"Search me, God, and know my _______________; test me and know my anxious _________________. See if there is any _______________________ __________ in me, and lead me in the way everlasting."

Our desire throughout this study is to allow ourselves to be led by God. Allowing God to search us and know us shows our desire not only to be honest but also to grow. Growth begins when we are honest about any burdens or junk that has crept into our lives. During our hectic days and sleepless nights, physical and emotional burdens can begin to take over our heart, thoughts, and mind. Knowing what specific issues we are dealing with will help us decide how to sort through it all. As we discover the burdens in our lives, we need to be intentional about not allowing guilt to take over. We're going to be honest while claiming the truth that God is leading us. He's the one putting us together in a fresh way, and we can trust him. It's time to be honest about our physical and emotional burdens while allowing God to search us to find anything offensive in our lives. Don't turn back now—this is when things get real and life-changing!

PHYSICAL BURDENS

These are the items that take up measured, actual space in your home. Whether they are packed in a box or sitting on a shelf, these burdens remain stagnant. They are present, but they don't have a particular function or usefulness. Not all physical things are bad. Some carry precious memories of times gone by and reminders of family and friends. The only time physical items turn into burdens is when they take up space that could be used and enjoyed by living, breathing people. If the physical "stuff" in our home limits the use of our actual living space, it needs to go. People come first, and the people living in our home have specific needs. If you are running out of room or feel stressed by the constant presence of useless items in your life, you have allowed the items to take over. Now, they are considered junk instead of precious. I know it sounds harsh. It can be difficult to part with items we feel an attachment to, but our goal is to have a home and a life that is put together in such a way that God is glorified and our family's needs are met.

Not all items start out as junk. Most things that find their way into our home come with intention and value, but the fact remains: they are taking up space. For example, I'm sure many of us have received gifts from our children that are precious but useless. (Honesty sometimes sounds very harsh, doesn't it?) The hand-painted flowerpot or noodle necklace are wonderful, but after a time they don't really hold a place of necessity in our lives. Kate, a mother of two girls, was desperate for an answer to this exact issue. She was more than willing to part with the gifts from her children, but her girls weren't so keen on the idea. If they saw a painting was missing or a gift was in the trash, they would become upset and Kate would begin to feel very guilty. In her desire to help her girls feel special, Kate was feeling overwhelmed and frustrated. I talked with Kate about some ideas and even some examples we've used in our home. She was eager to apply them to her situation, and I am happy to report that her girls' negative reactions have lessened and her house isn't as cluttered. Kate was able to put together a plan that worked for her because she was honest about the physical burden and asked for help.

Here's one of the ideas I shared with Kate: when my children bring me gifts or make a craft, I take a picture of my child holding the item they created. These pictures help me remember what my children looked like, how old they were, and what they made. Just for fun, I sometimes sneak into the picture too! By taking a picture, I have captured the moment without their creation turning into a potential burden taking up much-needed space in our home. I display their creations in specific areas: the back of a door, hanging on a magnet strip, posted on the fridge, or taped to my bathroom mirror. Having specific spaces assigned provides a natural limit to the amount of items that can be displayed. When one of my boys brings a new creation home, I let him know that we

NOTES

need to take the old item down to make room for the new. If anyone has hurt feelings or questions this action, I remind him that we have a picture too! I can show my children the picture and assure them I will *never* forget the effort they put into their gift. I do have one exception to this rule. When I am given a gift that has my boys' footprint or handprint on it, I keep the actual item and take a picture. These are so precious to me because they can't be re-created or replaced. I write the date, age, and child's name on the back and place them in a file folder I keep in the basement.

Can you think of any physical items that have been or might become burdens in your home? Maybe you are dealing with memorabilia, clothing, toys, or gifts you've been given. Whatever is lurking in your home, take a moment to write down its name—be as specific as you can. Being aware of these items and acknowledging their presence will help us remain accountable for dealing with them. We might not have time to sort everything out today, but when the opportunity comes to thin out our belongings, we will have a better sense of where to focus our attention.

Don't worry about coming up with a plan; we'll tackle those specifics in future chapters. For now, simply identify anything with physical properties that is taking up more space and energy than it is giving back.

Here are some verses to challenge us (no guilt, please!) as we seek a new perspective and learn how to deal with the physical burdens in our lives. Paul writes to his partner in ministry, Timothy, about what true contentment is. Paul had experienced two different ways to live life: one with Christ and one without. He knew better than anyone that nothing the physical world had to offer could compare to the grace, peace, and joy the Holy Spirit can bring to a life that is surrendered to God. Read **1 Timothy 6:6-9** and discover how Paul viewed earthly belongings and fill in the blanks on the next page.

"But godliness with ____________________

is great gain. For we ___________________

____________________ into the world,

and we can take nothing out of it. But if we

have food and clothing, we ____________

________ ____________________ with

that. Those who want to __________

______________ fall into temptation and

a trap and into many foolish and harmful

desires that plunge people into ____________

and destruction."

But godliness
with contentment
is great gain.
—1 Timothy 6:6

Sometimes a portion of Scripture is filled with multiple truths, all supporting a main theme. Each verse from our 1 Timothy scripture challenges us to be honest. They bring specific challenges and insights we can apply to our lives. Beginning with verse 6 and ending with verse 9, let's take a deeper look at how these words can be applied to our lives.

1 Timothy 6:6

When we go to church, pray at home, and are kind to everyone in the world, we are fulfilling the basic requirements of living a godly life. In verse 6, Paul challenges us to go beyond having only Christlike actions. He wants us to bring a spirit of contentment to our Christian walk. Being content allows us to experience a Christ-filled purpose that directly affects how we respond to life.

Have you experienced situations when you struggled to find contentment? Provide as much detail as you can about that particular event in the space below.

______

______

______

______

______

______

Did the situation change or did your heart change? What did you gain from enduring through this time?

______

______

______

______

______

It can be difficult to be honestly content with our situation, our home, and our belongings. Scripture promises that once we are content we will enjoy great gain. I hope what you gained from this time of reflection continues to spur you on to contentment in all areas of your life.

1 Timothy 6:7

Paul is quick to qualify what kind of "gain" we should seek: "For we brought nothing into the world, and we can take nothing out of it." When your first child came home with you, I'm certain the child was greeted with a myriad of possessions, each one waiting to care for and protect this sweet new baby. Our newborns bring nothing with them when they enter the world. Instead, we bring these items to them.

When you think about your children and what they truly need in order to thrive and be safe, what comes to mind?

Providing more than the basics is normal, wonderful, and in some cultures it is expected. When we are providing for our children, we need to examine the spirit and the attitude it creates in them. Are we encouraging our children to have a spirit of gratitude and contentment? Do our children understand the difference between the essentials of life and the extras? This is not an easy skill or perspective to instill in our family members, especially when they are surrounded by advertisements and technology that demand to be a part of their day. In future chapters, we'll discuss some specific approaches when dealing with technology, but for now, please write down any ideas you've used or have heard about to help children appreciate physical items and the purpose they serve. Writing out our thoughts on paper helps us remember how to reach for a "gain" that is valued in heaven and on earth.

1 Timothy 6:8

Paul makes a very bold statement in verse 8, sharing his perspective about what is essential and what is extra. He writes, "But if we have food and clothing, we will be content with that." During his time as an apostle of Christ, Paul was accustomed to being in prison, threatened, lied about, and misunderstood. Outside of these difficult moments, Paul helped establish some of the first churches and watched as entire communities found the joy that comes from walking with Christ.

I would love to declare that my relationship with God is so fulfilling that I'd be fine only having food and clothing. I wish I could say that having a home, pictures to hang on the wall, and my own bathroom aren't priorities in my life, but the truth is, they are important to me. Outside of a mission trip or community project, I really haven't been put in the position of surviving without these "extras."

NOTES

A family in our neighborhood endured a fire that destroyed their home. In a short twenty minutes every picture, every memory, everything sentimental was gone. I spoke to the mother of that family and even though the accident was years ago, she still gets tears in her eyes as she mourns the loss of some of those items, simply because they can never be replaced. Her tears begin to fade when she looks around and realizes her family is safe and they too could never be replaced. She has challenged me to keep my priorities focused on the people in my life and not allow the physical possessions to steal my energy or my joy.

If I have food, shelter, and clothing, I am blessed and I *can* be content. To search after more physical gain would only serve to undermine the true gifts in my life: my family members.

1 Timothy 6:9

In his letters to Timothy, Paul was very honest about what Timothy should and should not hold on to. Paul had seen greed and the things of this world overtake people's souls. He didn't want anyone who followed Christ to become a victim of Satan's lies. Paul writes, "Those who want to get rich fall into temptation and a trap and into many foolish and harmful desires that plunge people into ruin and destruction." Most people would never intentionally plunge themselves into ruin. However, if we are only seeking wealth and physical gain, these items can lead us down a path of slow, quiet destruction.

If we begin to serve credit cards, reward cards, and enticing sale bills, we can unknowingly start to serve physical items and money instead of them serving us. Financial strain begins when we convince ourselves we deserve an item or experience even though our bank account can't support that desire. When this happens, we see verse 9 come to life, and we can begin to feel as though everything is lost. Like a trapped animal, we start to strike out at anyone near us. Our families are usually on the receiving end of our stressful outbursts, and this kind of reality can indeed lead to the "destruction" Paul is talking about.

Jesus talked about this same kind of destruction with his disciples. He knew the limitations of human beings and the fact that we can easily be taken over by our desires. Discover Jesus' words in **Matthew 6:24** while filling in the missing words from this challenging and applicable verse.

"No one can serve _______ ______________. Either you will hate the one and love the other, or you will be _________________ to the one and despise the other. You cannot serve __________ God and ________________."

Since we can't serve both God and money, we have a choice to make. When we're concerned about discovering God more than we are about discovering the latest fashions, we'll experience the peace that God promises for our spirit. We cannot allow the things that sneak into our home to shift our priorities. In all honesty, we know people are more important than things, but do our actions reflect this sentiment? Take a moment to pray about any physical burdens or desires that could influence your ability to remain content and focused on God. As you pray, write down anything that comes to your mind. This time of waiting before the Lord is precious, and the thoughts you have are the result of the Holy Spirit showing you new ways to be put together.

____

____

____

____

I understand how uncomfortable it can be to talk about the physical burdens, including debt, weighing on us. Being honest isn't always a pleasant process, but it's essential to our well-being and growth. Look back at the items you identified as physical burdens on on page 42. Take a moment to prioritize them in order of which ones represent the most stress and/or burden in your life. If you feel comfortable, talk to friends about these issues and allow them to share any solutions you could use. Your honesty could potentially bring a sense of freedom and safety to others dealing with the same things. Remember: we're focusing on what is essential and striving to live a balanced life, all while gaining strength from God. These goals will become a reality when we dare to be honest.

EMOTIONAL BURDENS

Physical burdens are easily seen. Emotional burdens can be difficult to define and measure, but their weight and influence can't be denied. Two main components work together to influence how we presently deal with emotional burdens.

The first comes from how we were raised. Think back to your childhood to the people who most impacted your development. Did you observe emotions being expressed and processed, or were they repressed? Were people challenged to control their emotions, or were emotions allowed to control people and the situation? Write a short summary of what you were exposed to concerning emotional health and expression during your childhood and youth.

____

____

____

____

____

The second influencer springs from our personality today. Would you consider yourself an extrovert (you get energy from being with other people) or an introvert (you need time alone to recharge)? Perhaps your emotional needs and/or condition has changed since becoming a mom. Thinking about your view of the world and emotional needs, how would you describe your personality?

____

____

____

Most of us interchange the words "feelings" and "emotions" during our conversations. However, these terms carry specific definitions and have separate instigators. Feelings are typically defined as coming in response to an external event happening to us. For example, in our premarital counseling sessions we practiced saying things like, "When you do ____ it makes me feel like ___." On the other hand, emotions tend to emerge from within our being. They are present with or without an external event or influence. During our time together we're going to focus on the emotions we experience and how they affect our lives.

One morning I woke up in a very bad mood. I was still adjusting to my new life as a stay-at-home mom and, to be honest, I was resenting my role and the day of diapers, feedings, and laundry awaiting me. I didn't bother to pray or objectively think through my bitterness—instead I let my emotions overtake my thoughts. When our toddler spilled his drink, I became angry with him and brought him to tears with my words of frustration. Even in this moment I didn't have any compassion or sympathy—instead I became more agitated and blamed my children for my rotten attitude. When we allow our emotions to determine our state of mind, our state of mind affects our thoughts and our thoughts then influence the words we speak to others.

We've all had days when our emotions run wild and challenge our typically pleasant demeanor. Emotions can't be allowed to overtake us and have a negative influence. If given the chance, Satan can try to use our emotions to influence and control us. To demonstrate this situation, I've created an emotional equation to help us see the cause and effect of emotional burdens.

emotions left unchecked	+	a mind-set influenced by emotions	=	unguarded/hurtful comments and responses

Can you think of a situation when this emotional equation was a reality for you? If you can't, that's okay. Perhaps you remember a time when you've seen people in your life allow their emotions to overtake their mind and in turn they've spoken hurtful words or responded inappropriately. Being honest is tough, but honesty only works when you are able to accept the information being shared. Please know I would never want you to fabricate or share situations that make you uncomfortable or embarrassed. This is meant to help you grow—take as much time as you need. Thank you for being willing to share.

______________ + ______________ = ______________

emotions + mind-set = words/actions

For some of us, the tone of our day is set before our feet hit the ground. This tone is based on the emotions we are experiencing. If we give them permission, our emotions can take over our ability to function and interact with the world around us. Are emotions bad? No. Are emotions real? Yes. Are emotions reliable? Not at all! If I react out of emotion, I am guaranteed to go too far or mishandle a situation. When emotions are left unchecked, they can threaten to take over our mind-set and our day. During these moments we need to:

- ☑ Stop
- ☑ Take a deep breath
- ☑ Process what emotions are present
- ☑ Allow our rational mind to be in charge

Following these actions will help us react to and interact with people on a more rational and consistent level.

When we want to be honest with ourselves and with others, we want to make sure our emotions aren't the only things influencing us. **Galatians 5:16** helps us understand what it means to keep our responses in check and rely on the Holy Spirit to guide each word and emotion we encounter.

"So I say, ___________ by the ________________, and you will not __________________ the desires of the _______________."

Wow. I think about my typical day, read the words "walk by the Spirit," and I suddenly feel like asking for a do-over! It's difficult to live out verse 16 when our flesh gets in the way. Even when we're exhausted, hurried, or overwhelmed, we have to make a choice to set negative emotions aside and not gratify the desires of the flesh. When we choose to do this, a spilled drink changes from the most difficult, irritating, and unwelcome event in our day to what it really is: an accident. Our families need to know that our emotions won't manage us; we will manage and control our emotions. When this is practiced, we are working hard to walk by the Spirit and allow him to do a new work in our lives.

Let's make a new equation patterned after the challenge from Galatians. When we walk by the Spirit we can manage our emotions in a new way.

emotions come + prayers go up to ask for help = Holy Spirit strengthens us and provides a fresh perspective

At times, I have allowed my emotions to determine my responses, and those were not my finest parenting moments. I've had to apologize to my children for overreacting or for punishing them with my mood because of something that happened at work. I never apologize for having an emotion, but I do apologize for allowing those emotions to determine my actions and reactions.

Please understand I'm not suggesting we shouldn't feel anything, or that we should deny our emotions. I believe each thought and emotion we experience can produce moments when our faith matures and our self-control grows. This can only happen when our emotional responses and the emotions that enter into our day come under the direct power and influence of the Holy Spirit. Emotions don't need to go away, but they do need to be kept in check. It's an exhausting process, but we aren't alone in learning how to deal with our emotive selves. God promised to be with us and help us each step of the way.

Whether we're dealing with physical or emotional burdens, we can have confidence that nothing can separate us from God's Spirit and his helping hand. Read this promise Moses shared with his successor, Joshua, in **Deuteronomy 31:8**:

> "The LORD himself ____________ ______________ you and will be with you; he will never leave you nor forsake you. Do not be ____________; do not be ________________________."

Whatever burdens or issues come our way, we don't need to fear. We aren't afraid to ask honest questions and hear honest answers. We know the Lord God himself has gone before us, and he's with us each day. He'll never leave us, forget about us, or ask us to fend for ourselves.

If we're honest with each other and with ourselves, we'll discover we have a lot in common. We all have struggles, joys, burdens, and fears. The next time you're with a group of fellow moms, I challenge you to be honest and share a bit about what's going on in your heart and your life. Your honesty might be the key to unlocking the grip fear has on so many mothers.

CLOSING PRAYER

Lord, help me see the burdens in my life for what they really are and surrender them completely. I ask that your cleansing and healing Spirit would move in my life. I don't want to keep going through the motions. I want to see how you are putting my physical and emotional life together in a new way. Help me to be aware of others around me and any burdens they might be carrying. Thank you for the reminder that what we own here on earth is nothing compared to the riches waiting for us in heaven. Lord, help my heart to treasure what is important to you. Remove any pride or ego from me, Lord. Thank you for never leaving me and for always being with me. I determine here and now to not be afraid or discouraged. I love you, Lord. Amen.

4

MIRROR, MIRROR ON THE WALL

Mom Essential: IDENTITY

MOM MOMENT

Matthew 5:13*a*-14*a*: "You are the salt of the earth. . . . You are the light of the world."

I was eight years old when I first heard the phrase "mirror, mirror on the wall." Having a magic mirror might be nice, but unlike Snow White's stepmother, I wouldn't ask about beauty. I'd say, "Mirror, mirror in front of my face, tell me the truth and add a little grace." To which my mirror would answer something like, "Makeup is overrated and sweat-pants are all the rage" or "Ordering pizza means you'd rather spend time with your children than your oven and the oven doesn't mind one bit."

If I felt really brave, I might ask my mirror who the best mom was and I think it would have an answer. In my mind the mirror would pause for a moment, show my reflection, and say, "The best mom is the one you are today—the one who learned from yesterday's mistakes and looks forward to growing with her children during each tomorrow she is blessed to enjoy." Perhaps I imagine my mirror to be a bit philosophical, but it would have to reserve these comments for days when I was well-rested and well-fed so I could take it all in!

No one is perfect. There is no magic formula or mirror to help us connect with our identity. At one time or another, most of us will battle against the temptation to base our identity on what we do as a mom instead of who we are as a Christian woman. We hold multiple titles, but our identity should be found solely in who we are as a child of God. When I claim my status as a child, I begin to see life in a new way and discover a sense of freedom in my spirit.

Acting as a "child," I'm allowed to enjoy the process of growing, learning, and discovering everything around me, much like toddlers explore the world around them.

Before becoming a mom, I could look in the mirror and clearly define my identity. I was a teacher, wife, daughter, friend, and child of God. If I'm being honest, I also felt as though I had complete control of my life and what happened throughout my day. During my first week home with our son, I realized I had a lot to learn and life had plenty it wanted to teach me. It was in those moments of not being in control and not having all the answers that I rediscovered what it meant to exercise a "childlike" faith. (See **Matthew 18:3**.) I was forced to align my identity with my Creator instead of my earthly roles.

Before you became a parent, how would people have identified you? By your career, education, social involvement, or other areas?

____

____

____

Being a child of God has its benefits. Our heavenly Father cares about every detail and aspect of our lives, both small and big. He cares about our day. God recognizes and identifies with each emotion, frustration, and accomplishment we encounter as we go through this journey. We know our Father is with us. No matter what happens, we can sense his presence and peace. My response to this outpouring of love comes when I trust my heavenly Father to rearrange, redefine, or perhaps remove anything (or anyone) that has a negative impact on my identity.

Each of us experienced a before and after concerning motherhood. There was a specific season of growth each of us experienced before we became mothers. The length of time and the events that occurred might be different, but I truly believe God begins his "good work" in us long before we are entrusted with our children. If God began the work before we were moms, he is sure to continue that process.

When we read **Philippians 1:3-11**, we discover some key phrases that will help us understand the "big" picture involving our identity in Christ and his plan for our lives. Read through these verses and take note of the following words as you read. I have them underlined in my Bible because they bring me such peace and joy.

"pray with joy"
"being confident"
"depth of insight"
"discern what is best"
"to the glory and praise of God"

Identity is the last essential we'll study under the theme of being "put together" for God's glory. We've tackled some tough questions and challenged ourselves in some fairly sensitive areas. Our first essential, balance, brought the challenge of making Scripture reading and prayer essential parts of our lives. Have you found yourself able to "pray with joy" more regularly or perhaps use Scripture to bring balance to a difficult situation? Think of a specific instance or perhaps a new routine that's helped you stay connected to Scripture and enjoying an active prayer life. Record these details below.

Balance

Studying these ten essentials won't do us any good if we don't apply them. By making minor adjustments within our daily lives, we will see major shifts in our spiritual growth.

Through this growth, we begin to see our identity through God's Word instead of through the world's eyes. Our desire to be salt and light to this dark and sinful world requires us to be women who are strong. In Philippians we read that we should "be confident." We know confidence in the world or in ourselves will not bring us the kind of strength we need. Have you discovered a new or renewed source of strength? Take a moment to give God praise and thanks for helping you find and claim a renewed sense of strength that brings you confidence.

By making minor adjustments within our daily lives, we will see major shifts in our spiritual growth.
#MomEssentials

Strength

Along with the essentials of balance and strength, we've been challenged to be honest. When we are honest about our situation and how we see God putting us together, we avoid having any sort of false identity. Has God revealed any new or recurring issues in your life that might sneak up and influence how you define yourself and your role as a mom?

Honesty

> *Who we are should be a direct reflection of whose we are.*
> #MomEssentials

I think the most honest moments for me occur before I go to bed and when I wake up. In the evening I look back over my day, and sometimes I'm quite pleased with everything. Other times, I wonder where the day went. This is when I remember that who I am is not defined by what I accomplish. Nope. Not at all. If I relied on my ability to complete all the tasks on my to-do lists to define my identity, I would never find it. I don't think those lists ever stop being made! This is where our "depth of insight" becomes invaluable. Our inward and outward perspective of self begins to evolve. When I look in the mirror, I see that I am a mother to my children, and that title involves more than can be seen in the physical realm of my day.

One day I was at the park with my boys. A former co-worker I hadn't seen in years was also there. I asked what she was doing now and her answer shocked me. She looked down at the ground with a sort of apologetic sigh and said, "Oh, I'm just staying home with these little monsters." I was speechless (but only for a short moment—this is a rare thing for me). Our Philippians scripture beckons us to "discern what is best." Each mother and situation is unique. When we do what we discern is best for our family, we can stand confident in our role and our responsibilities. We need to love ourselves, our family, and our calling to be a mom to our kids.

You see, we're all working mothers. Some of us have to leave our house to fulfill our job, while others have their office in their home. What do you need in your life in order for you to be a balanced, productive person? Discerning what is best for our family cultivates a genuine identity that is secure no matter what "job" we have. Each of us can be salt and light to this world whether we're in a boardroom or at a playground. Both are mission fields and provide opportunities for us to give God praise for helping us remain put together each day. The most important aspect of our identity is that it brings glory to God our Creator. The last phrase we highlighted from our Philippians scripture ("to the glory and praise of God") reminds us that *who* we are should be a direct reflection of *whose* we are. We are God's children. We are his creation, and he made us in *his* image! How does seeing yourself as a "child of God" impact your identity as a mother? How can you become a child of God while raising children and grandchildren?

Identity

Living as God's child instead of "Ashley and Michael's mom" can be challenging. When our children are young, we may feel like the world revolves around nap time, feeding time, and bedtime. As our children grow, the routine of life becomes even more chaotic with friends, technology, extracurricular events, school, and hormones.

As a parent, I need to allow God to put me together in a new way during each season of my life. I have no business trying to create a false identity or pretend I already know everything. Keeping a tidy home and caring for our families are part of our reality and calling. But we also need to look at the big picture and remember why our responsibilities matter. Read all of Psalm 127 and use the space provided to rewrite these verses in your own words. How do you interpret the promises found in these scriptures?

"I must realize that my obedience, even in the smallest detail of life, has all of the omnipotent power of the grace of God behind it."[1]

–Oswald Chambers

#MomEssentials

According to **Psalm 127:1**, "Unless the ________ builds the ________, the builders labor in ________." When our identities are aligned with being children of God, we can be certain the Lord is building through us and we are not laboring in vain. We must guard our hearts against thinking the tasks we complete each day are somehow mundane or forgotten. I believe with all my heart that every meal we make, each room we organize, and each project we complete has the power of the Lord God Almighty behind it. The *Lord* is building our house through us. What an honor to partner with him! Believing that God is in every detail of our day brings a new sense of purpose and importance to our role as caretaker of our house.

Verse 2 continues with the promise of something very precious to a mom, sleep. Fill in the missing words from **Psalm 127:2**:

> "In ____________ you rise early and stay up
>
> ____________, toiling for food to eat—for he
>
> grants ________________ to those he loves."

Before anyone rushes home to claim exemption from fixing any more meals or cleaning, let's look a little closer at the message behind this verse. I've known women who stay up until one or two o'clock in the morning cleaning their houses. If this habit is continued on a regular basis, these women begin to feel exhausted purely from their lack of sleep. The desire to have a clean home is wonderful, but when it drives us to sacrifice our health, this desire can stem from a root of vanity.

Are we trying to create a "perfect mom" identity by having a perfectly clean house and perfectly ordered home? This vain spirit is seen when we place a clean house ahead of our family. When we are too tired to care for our children because we spent all our energy taking care of our house, it is clear where our priorities lie. Verse 2 of Psalm 127 says that God will give sleep to those he loves. We know our God loves us, but do we believe he approves of us if our house is dirty? God can help us find rest whether everything on our list is checked off or left for another day. When our identity isn't wrapped up in, or defined by, the condition of our house, we have the freedom to stop toiling and start resting.

Some of the neighborhoods near us have an event called "The Parade of Homes." People can sign up to tour these houses that have been deemed unique, beautiful, and special. I've been inside some of these model homes, and I must say, I was impressed! But as I walked on the shiny floors and enjoyed the light streaming through the perfectly clean windows, I had a revelation. I was looking at a house, not a home.

I've begun to realize that a home where children reside is a space marked by finger-printed windows, stained carpet, and at least one pile of toys or clothes that never seem to find a permanent home. I'll admit it—I love having a clean house. But I don't toil and clean so people will identify me as the best homemaker ever. I maintain our home so it can be a house where I enjoy my reward and my children.

Take a moment to write down the name of each person in your house in the space below. Next to each name, write a short description of how you help take care of him or her and meet his or her needs.

My Family

NOTES

In case you haven't heard it today, "Thank you for taking care of your house and your family. You are amazing!" As moms, our identity can begin to feel tarnished and/or limited by our daily routines and activities, but did you know you are doing the work of the kingdom of heaven? Yes, ma'am, you are.

Jesus knew not everyone was called to be full-time missionaries, preachers, or teachers. But he knew everyone could make a difference. Jesus wanted us to know that God notices and appreciates our efforts, no matter how small they might seem to the outside world. In Matthew 25, we hear Jesus explaining how God will recognize his "sheep" or his "followers" when he returns to earth on judgment day. Read **Matthew 25:31-40** and complete the final verse and its missing words.

> "The King will reply, 'Truly I tell you, whatever you did for ________ ________ ________ ____________ of these brothers and sisters of mine, you did for ________'" (v. 40).

There are many groups of people that would qualify as "the least of these" in our world. Starving children in Africa, the homeless, prisoners, widows—the list goes on and on. But in my world right now, my "least of these" are my family members. I want to be identified as a "sheep," as a follower of Christ who ministers to those who need me. One day I might be able to travel the globe and help those suffering from poverty and hunger. For now I'm going to feed my children, try to keep them clothed, and teach them how to make their own breakfast.

I don't mean to trivialize what we do with humor, but I think it's important to remember that God has called us to be ministers in our home and to do our work with a joyful heart, even if that work seems mundane and repetitive. You and I are making a difference, and we are modeling our Savior's actions.

Those of us with older children know that age doesn't lessen their dependence on us. They don't need our physical help as much as they desire a spiritual, intellectual, and emotional connection. Jesus was very patient with his clueless disciples. We can follow his lead and extend a servant heart to our teens and adult children when we're closely identified with our Savior.

Record what action Jesus performed in **John 13:1-17**:

____

____

Simon Peter understood that Jesus was God's Son. This knowledge made it difficult for him to understand why Jesus would wash someone's feet. This job was done by the lowliest of servants and wasn't pleasant. But Jesus reminded his disciples that they were to follow his example. The next time you do something "small" for your family, I hope you'll remember this quote from Oswald Chambers' *My Utmost for His Highest*:

> If I will do my duty, not for duty's sake but because I believe God is engineering my circumstances, then at the very point of my obedience all of the magnificent grace of God is mine through the glorious atonement by the Cross of Christ.[2]

We do a thousand little things each day, and some of them can be seen and measured. Other tasks we complete will only be seen through our children's lives as they grow, but God is in each moment along the way. No matter the task, each one brings with it the omnipotent power and superb grace of God. Please read **1 John 3:1-2** and fill in the missing words from these verses:

"See what great __________ the Father has _________________ on us, that we should be called __________________ of God! And that is what we are! The reason the world does not __________ us is that it did not know him. Dear friends, now we are _________________ of God, and what we will _______ has not yet been made known."

Each day we need to remember the last statement from our 1 John scripture, "What we will be has not yet been made known." We will always be a mom, no matter the age of our children. But if you have young children, you need to remember that beyond the diapers, laundry, and meals, God is putting your life together for something greater than you could ever imagine! We might not know the end result, but God does. In the meantime, we must recognize how our service to our family identifies us with the servant heart of Christ.

As believers, we understand that our greatest strength source—God—created us, and we can be honest about the traits and qualities he put into our being. As women, we should be proud of our gender and the many roles we fulfill. My prayer is that a woman's role in the home, workplace, and society as a whole would be equally recognized and appreciated. The world might not know God, but they do know us. We have an amazing opportunity to show the world who God is through our lives.

Trust your Father in heaven and enjoy claiming your identity as a child of God. Our identity is formed as Christ works in us to accomplish his purpose of bringing his love and light to this broken world. I hope you enjoy the freedom that comes from living in the shadow of God's grace and mercy. He isn't judging us—he's cheering for us! I think if we asked our magic mirror to comment on our identity, it would answer back, "Keep being salt and light as you raise the next generation of moms and dads that will change the world. And by the way, you rock at it!"

CLOSING PRAYER

Dear heavenly Father, help me see my daily responsibilities and accomplishments as more than just items checked off a to-do list. Help me find my identity in you and not in my accomplishments. Lord, I dedicate my house and my family to you. Use my life to further your kingdom. Give me the strength to be honest with others as I give you glory for what you are doing in my life. Thank you for allowing me to rest, even when everything isn't put away or clean. Thank you for blessing me with the title of "mom." I need your power and grace to help me, and I thank you for being a faithful God who sees and meets my needs. I trust you, Lord, and I know that just as you've called me to serve you and our family, you will help me along the way. I give you all the praise and honor, Lord! Amen.

THEME 2

H SHAPED UP

5

MOM MOMENT

Isaiah 43:19*a*: "See, I am doing a new thing!"

EXTREME MOM MAKEOVER

Mom Essential: GROWTH

Reality shows can sometimes go too far, while others bring a perspective that is truly life-changing. My favorite part of makeover shows is the reveal. Sometimes the reveal happens after hair, makeup, and wardrobe have been finalized and the person sees his or her reflection for the first time. Other reveals happen when family members see their loved one in an entirely new light.

No matter the audience, seeing ourselves in a new way can be shocking, amazing, and downright surprising. As we continue on this journey together, I pray your time of study has offered a chance for God to reveal something to you. Has God been putting you together in a new way? Were you able to discover Scripture in a new way? Take a moment to reflect on the essentials we've focused on so far. How have they impacted your prayer life and daily activities?

I hope you've felt encouraged while gaining fresh insight into how God is putting you together as a mom. Perhaps your home, your heart, or your relationships are finding new ways to be put together. No matter the area, bravo to you for being faithful in responding to God's leading! Chapters 5, 6, and 7 support the second theme for our time together: Shaped Up. Get ready to sweat it out and work hard. The more you put in, the more you'll get out of this time!

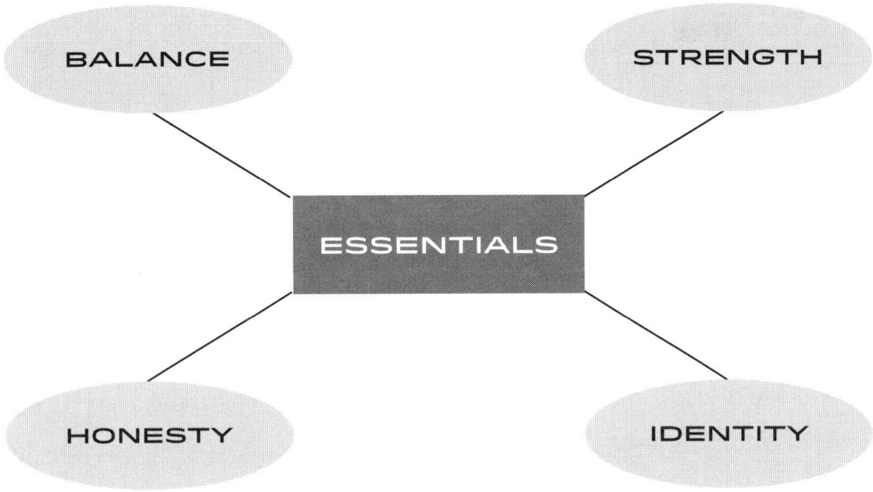

Allowing God to shape or reshape our lives isn't easy. Admitting we aren't perfect and that we sometimes need help takes determination and commitment. Once we allow God to show us what pieces need to be in place for our lives to be whole, he can begin shaping us into the kind of woman and mother he wants us to be. The process of being shaped might not sound like fun, but when we allow God to shape our spirit and mind, he can create something wonderful and complete in us. Before we move on, look back at our Mom Moment for this chapter. Fill in the missing words from Isaiah 43:19*a*:

"See, _____ am doing a __________ thing!"

In response to this scripture, who is doing a new thing in our lives? ___________ Although our relationship with Christ is a partnership, we need to recognize that *God* is working in our lives to prepare us for *his* purpose. This realization doesn't give us license to sit back and release our personal responsibility; in fact, it does just the opposite. When we understand God is the one shaping us, we begin to respond to his leading and accept the growth his presence brings.

Discovering what "new thing" God is doing can be exciting, frightening, and sometimes unnerving. No matter the emotions involved in this process, we'll have a better understanding of what "new thing" God is doing when we continue to apply our commitment from chapter 1 to pray and read Scripture.

Throughout Scripture, we read how Jesus changed people's lives and met them in their moment of need. I think one of the most unique and wonderful miracles Jesus performed can be found in the book of Mark. It's a fantastic story of faith, healing, and, well, spit. Let's discover how Jesus did a new thing for a deserving man by reading **Mark 7:31-37** and completing the missing information from these verses.

After the people begged for Jesus to heal the man, what did Jesus do first? ____. When I read how Jesus responded to the people he met, I immediately feel a check in my spirit. The simple act of Jesus taking "him aside, away from the crowd" reminds me that Jesus was here doing God's work. At no time did he seek recognition or praise. Jesus did everything with a humble heart and as a servant to his Father. Each time we read about Jesus ministering to and healing the people around him, we are drawn into an amazing, unique, and purposeful makeover story. The individuals within each story help us connect with and respond to Jesus' actions. The Bible is full of colorful, flawed, and amazing characters—just like the man in Mark's story. I love the details Mark provides. I can almost see the scene playing out in front of me.

I imagine the men in their long robes, Jesus' arm around the man's shoulder, dust stirring at their feet as they move away from the crowd of people. I'm certain the man wondered what Jesus had in store for him, and I'm sure the people wondered why they couldn't have a front row seat to watch Jesus work.

As we read further in Mark 7 we find Jesus' actions a bit odd, especially when we think about the environment surrounding him. While reading verses 33 and 34, write down each step Jesus carried out during this miracle of healing.

____

____

____

____

To be honest, the thought of someone sticking his fingers in my ears makes me feel a bit uncomfortable. Can you imagine what the man was thinking at this point? With his thoughts still spinning, the man then watched Jesus spit into his own hand and reach to open the man's mouth (remember, this man is deaf and mute, but not blind). Call me a wimp, but the thought of allowing my tongue to be touched by unwashed, dirty fingers almost takes me over the edge.

After enduring such unconventional treatment, our character heard what was undoubtedly the most beautiful word this man had ever heard. He'd never heard a bird sing, children laughing, or his mother's voice, but in this sweet moment he heard the voice of Jesus as he spoke the command *"Ephphatha!"* This means "Be opened!" Jesus was calling for the man's sense of hearing to be active and for his ears to be opened.

The deaf and mute man we meet in Mark 7 had to endure some fairly bizarre behavior from our Savior, but Jesus deemed each of those actions as necessary in order to heal the man. To help us identify each detail of the story, try to remember the seven actions that occurred (the first and last have been done for you):

1. Jesus took him aside.

2. ______________________________

3. ______________________________

4. ______________________________

5. ______________________________

6. ______________________________

7. The man's ears were opened and tongue loosened, and he began to speak plainly.

Now that we have all the elements to our story, we can start applying them to our own lives. Isn't that why we're here? We get to watch, front and center, as God shapes our lives through the miracle his Son performed so long ago. This is growth at the most exciting and useful level. I hope this idea thrills you as much as it does me! Jesus shaped this man's experience through multiple steps, and I believe each one carried with it an opportunity for the man to refuse or run away from Christ. Instead, the man endured. He trusted God. We can follow this example as we allow God to shape us, mold us, and in the end, provide the best and most-needed makeover we've ever experienced.

TOOK HIM ASIDE

As mothers, we have a lot on our plates. The hours in our day are filled with good things, but the fact remains that each hour is indeed full. God isn't pushy. Instead, he's patient. He won't barge into our lives and demand our attention. It's amazing to me that the God who created the universe and told the sun and stars where to go isn't going to barge into my life and tell me what to do. Instead he asks me to simply knock, and he will answer. I'm to seek him and know I'll find him. (See **Luke 11:9**.)

Seeking means we are responsible for making room in our schedules for Christ, even if that time looks different than it did before we had children. I've discovered some of the most ordinary activities like mowing the lawn, vacuuming, or folding laundry can bring extraordinary moments with my Lord. One mom I met in Colorado makes a habit of praying for each of her four children by name as she folds their clean clothes. She prays for the activities they'll enjoy and the people they will meet while wearing the outfits she is putting away.

Cyndi, a mom to two young children, has a kitchen window that looks out onto her neighborhood. When she stands in front of her sink Cyndi prays for her neighbors and takes time to listen to the Lord. She might be able to read Scripture and pray again during the day, but if you ever see Cyndi at her sink, you know she is not only helping dishes become clean—she is cleansing her soul too!

Washing dishes, doing laundry—it all seems ordinary. But when did we decide that God is only allowed to work in our spirit when we're at church or surrounded by music and other believers? God can work anytime, anywhere, as long as he is invited in.

If you currently have quiet time with God or if you are hoping to make this part of your routine, take a moment to write down when, how, and where God can have you all to himself and take you aside for a moment:

Lord, I'm yours!

Take heart, my sweet sister in Christ—you are doing an amazing job balancing everything in your life! I know it can seem overwhelming to think about adding one more activity into our day, but perhaps we can find a task that requires our hands to be busy but will let our heart and mind commune with God. Setting aside time for God is the first step toward our goal of having a body, mind, and spirit that is shaped into the image of our heavenly Father. (See Matthew 5:48.)

"Whether you turn to the right or to the left, your ears will hear a voice behind you, saying, 'This is the way; walk in it.'"
—Isaiah 30:21

PUT HIS FINGERS IN THE MAN'S EARS

Have you ever seen children stick their fingers in their ears, attempting to block out noise? Whether it's a loud sound or a request to comply, children can try almost everything to keep from hearing something that isn't pleasant. As juvenile as it might seem, I believe we sometimes plug our ears when it comes to spiritual matters. Maybe God is asking you to release an expectation you have of others or a responsibility you've taken on that has become a burden. Perhaps the impossible would seem possible if you could spend more time with the Lord and hear his voice a bit more clearly.

Even as adults we need to take our fingers out of our proverbial "ears" and really listen to God. By removing our stubbornness or busyness, some of us will be better able to hear his soft voice, maybe for the first time. It's a beautiful moment when we discover the gentle whisper of the Holy Spirit as he leads us through our day. When we are able to really hear, we also begin to listen more to other people. This is a beautiful practice because it reminds us that we aren't the only ones with needs or difficulties. Our ability to hear others releases us from a prison of selfish thoughts and ambitions.

The man in our story was deaf. He'd never heard a sound, not even the sound of his own breath. After Jesus opened this man's ears, he was given the gift of hearing the world around him, but Jesus didn't stop there. He also gave the man the ability to speak clearly and understand what the people around him were saying. Our God goes beyond our physical needs; he takes care of our spirit too. All we have to do is let him show us how to listen, and we'll discover truths and sounds we've never heard before. We might even gain a whole new perspective about our lives and how to deal with any difficulties or issues we are facing. What a wonderful reality to strive for—to hear things in a new way and speak with new words.

What does the promise from **Isaiah 30:21** mean to you when it comes to listening to God?

Lord, I'm listening!

HE SPIT

As a mother to three boys, I have to admit that "spit" is a subject I talk about more than I'd like. It all started with baseball. Before that point, my boys never would have even thought about spitting on the ground. Everything changed when they began watching, playing, and becoming part of the baseball world. I've come to a compromise of sorts with the males in my family. Spitting is now only acceptable when they are in the dugout or on the field. During all other occasions, swallow!

I grew curious about where Jesus spit and why he did. Spitting seemed like such a random and unnecessary action. According to *Matthew Henry's Commentary on the Whole Bible*, Jesus spit on his own finger before touching the man's tongue. Henry suggests Jesus did this in an effort to moisten the man's mouth and loosen whatever was keeping his tongue tied.[1]

Henry goes on to write that the actions Christ chose were a clear example that it was Jesus' "own *fingers* that he put into his ears, and his own *spittle* that he put upon his tongue; for he alone heals."[2] Wow! Jesus alone can heal! No amount of striving, good deeds, or bargaining can accomplish what Jesus can do in our lives when we allow him to touch us. Can I get an "amen"?

I never thought of spit as being a spiritual element, and in its own right, it isn't spiritual at all. But in our desire to focus on the essentials and how God is shaping us to be his follower, we might spit a little. Jesus added his spit to help the man begin to speak and his tongue to work. What do we need to add or do in order to experience a healing from our own emotional or physical burdens and experience growth? (See chapter 3.)

Maybe we need to speak openly about our issues for the first time. When we speak honestly, we must be willing to listen to someone else's perspective and suggestions for dealing with these things. You've heard the phrase, "Just spit it out"? Perhaps an honest conversation with someone we love and trust will help us "digest" what is really happening. However we decide to respond to God's leading, we must realize that this time of being shaped into who God wants us to be, for his purpose, can sometimes be a very messy, dirty process. But in the end we will be free from the junk that has kept us from hearing and speaking the truth concerning God's call on our lives and how he is helping us grow.

Lord, I'm being honest with you ...

HE TOUCHED THE MAN'S TONGUE

Our middle son, Tyler, was a very quiet child. By utilizing baby sign language, we were able to communicate with him. As he grew, I noticed Tyler was a little too quiet. I shared my concerns with other moms. They assured me he was quiet because

"We all stumble in many ways. Anyone who is never at fault in what they say is perfect, able to keep their whole body in check. When we put bits into the mouths of horses to make them obey us, we can turn the whole animal. Or take ships as an example. Although they are so large and are driven by strong winds, they are steered by a very small rudder wherever the pilot wants to go. Likewise, the tongue is a small part of the body, but it makes great boasts. Consider what a great forest is set on fire by a small spark."

—James 3:2-5

his older brother was speaking for him. As time passed and his verbal skills failed to develop, it was clear something was wrong.

After completing some tests, our questions were answered. Our son wasn't talking because he couldn't hear us. After surgery to correct the issue, I watched my little boy sit wide-eyed in a restaurant. He was trying to process and keep up with the myriad of sounds surrounding him. It was amazing to watch Tyler's world open up before him, but our journey wasn't over. You see—he could hear, but he still wasn't talking.

A therapist came to our house every week and worked with Tyler to help him make his own sound in a very noisy world. During one of our sessions I watched as the therapist asked Tyler to hold his tongue with his fingers and make a raw, guttural sound from his throat. I asked her why this was necessary. She explained, "Sometimes our tongue just gets in the way. By holding it still, a new sound can be made." She was a very wise woman.

When my son's sessions were finished, our therapist warned me that I should be prepared to discover a whole new side of his personality and will. When Tyler learned how to use his voice, he started speaking for himself. I have to admit—he has made up for any time he lost. Out of our three children, Tyler has the most to say, and he isn't afraid to share his thoughts and ideas. His tongue is working fine, and it is a powerful tool.

I am humbled and a bit ashamed when I think about how many burdens I've created because my tongue and my words got in the way. The book of James gives some wonderful examples of how powerful our tongue can be. Have you ever had a moment when your words created issues in your mind or in someone else's life? Being a teacher and speaker, I find myself praying that God would guard my tongue more than any other part of my body.

When we give our tongue free reign, it can be a destructive weapon. God wants to touch our tongue and reshape the words it creates. Under the control of the Holy Spirit, our words and our tongue can be shaped into tools that build others up and create an environment of hope and healing.

Take a moment to read through **James 3:2-5**.

After reflecting on the scripture from James, pray that God would help your tongue and the words you speak fulfill this command from **Colossians 4:6**:

> "Let your conversation be always full of ______________, seasoned
>
> with ___________, so that you may know how to answer everyone."

Thinking back to situations you've encountered, ask yourself if your conversations have been or are filled with grace and seasoned with salt. Using the chart, record general or specific moments and how you responded. Reflect on any situations when your tongue (words) helped or hurt the people in your life.

Taming the Tongue

Moments when my words helped	Moments when my words hurt
Action plan to have words full of grace	

LOOKED UP TO HEAVEN

We've been walking through the steps Jesus took to heal the man in our story. Take a moment and picture the timeline with me: first, Jesus takes the man off to the side; then, sticks his fingers in the man's ears; spits on his finger; touches the man's tongue; and finally he looks up. There's no doubt in my mind that this man was closely watching every move Jesus made. I can only assume that when Jesus looked up to heaven, the man looked up too. Here were two men, standing in the desert, looking up to heaven in expectation and wonder. By looking up, Jesus once again directs this man's eyes and our spirit to the fact that God alone can heal and provide.

Only through our Savior's intervention can we be truly successful in any endeavor we undertake. Whether we are cleaning out our basement or apologizing for emotional damage we may have caused, we need God's help! He alone can shape us into a beautiful creation. God has promised to stick with us throughout the entire growth and shaping process. He never tires of us. Our heavenly Father only asks us to look to him for direction and instruction. **Hebrews 10:23** commands us to:

"Hold unswervingly to the ____________ we profess, for he who promised is ________________."

Through our relationship with Christ we have a hope the world cannot replicate. Sometimes the secular world is truly confused by the strength and peace we can have during difficult times. Holding tightly to our faith and professing our hope points the world's eyes up to heaven. When the situations in our lives become difficult or our energy begins to falter, we only need to look up, hold on to our hope, and know that *he is faithful!*

Is God reshaping something in your life? Has life become difficult? Take a moment to write down the situation or issues you're facing.

Lord, I look to you!

SAID "BE OPENED"

Multiple times during my parenting career, I've prayed for God to open my eyes and help me see my children the way *he* sees them. I want to hear them like God hears them and share as many moments with them as I can. Sometimes I can get so overwhelmed with the activities in our lives that I forget to really listen and see my kids.

One day at playgroup, my friend Candi helped open my eyes and ears to what was right in front of me. We were sitting on a park bench, watching our kids play. I should clarify that Candi was the only one of us actually watching. I was too busy focusing on how tired I was and mourning the loss of my identity as a professional in the workforce. Smiling from ear to ear, Candi tapped my knee and stared off toward the sandbox. "Look at them, Kasey," she said. "Aren't they just amazing?! How they play together in their own little world. These days are so precious and they are going by so fast!"

I blinked back the tears as my eyes and my spirit were opened to what was really happening in front of me. I was missing beautiful moments and memories because I was focused on what I used to have. I was sitting there complaining to God, unaware of the wonderful gifts sitting right in front of me. I had closed myself off from seeing what really mattered, and my friend opened a new world for me.

Certain commentaries suggest Jesus let out a sigh before he spoke the word "ephphatha" into the heavens. He wasn't irritated or overwhelmed, but he was truly concerned about the new temptations and sins the man would be exposed to now that his speech was restored.[3] The ability to speak can be a blessing and a burden. Refer back to our scripture from James 3. James gives us two clear examples concerning the power of our tongue. Complete the following phrases according to the examples given in James 3:2-5.

Horses obey because of the _________ in their mouth.

A ship is steered by a ____________________.

A bit and a rudder are very small objects compared to the horse and boat they control. Although the tongue is a small part of our body, it can play a huge role in shaping our relationships. God's been in the tongue-taming, speech-shaping business since the beginning of time.

Before Jesus healed the man in our New Testament story, God was opening mouths and guiding speech. Moses was a very insecure man, doubting his abilities and afraid of the unknown. God called Moses to lead the Hebrew people out of captivity from Egypt, and Moses wasn't interested in fulfilling this role. What did God say to Moses in Exodus 4:10-12?

____

____

____

Some of us understand Moses better than we might like to admit, especially when it comes to our abilities. Like Moses, we begin to doubt our ability to be the mom, wife, co-worker, friend, or sister we hope to be. These insecurities come when the connection we have with our Creator is out of shape. God said he would help and teach Moses, and God used different situations to open Moses' eyes to this truth. That same God is reaching out to us each day, and asking us to trust him. He's here to help us grow and shape us into the women he made us to be. Using the space provided, write down any areas of your life that could use some growth—things like work, marriage, financial issues, and so on. Next to each area, write down what specific area or perspectives need to be reshaped by God's patient and kind hands.

AREA	SHAPING

Whether you wrote about a relationship or a responsibility, God knows your heart and each detail involved in the situation. Perhaps our tongues have gotten in the way and created rifts in relationships. Some of us are still struggling to believe God can use us, just as we are. Our willingness to invite God into our lives and allow him to show us how to grow means we will always be getting better, learning something new as we continue to move forward.

I would much rather be a person moving forward than being stagnant. The process of being shaped up cannot begin until growth takes place. A life shaped by God's grace carries a beautiful truth with it. This truth is lived out when we see our insecurities becoming assets because the power of God Almighty is with us, shaping us with each step we take. Through Scripture, we know God is faithful. We've seen time and time again how he fulfills his promises. So now it's our turn. We must accept the responsibility of being a child of God and take the first step toward growth becoming a reality, not just a goal.

Thinking back to the areas you wrote down, are there some steps you need to take to help this process begin? Take a moment to listen to the Holy Spirit. Ask God who or what you can connect with in order to ensure he can move in your life, continuing to help you grow. Space has been given on the next page if you'd like to write down any specific goals, plans, or actions that come to your mind. Remember—this is not a time to feel guilty; it is a time to enjoy the freedom that comes from honesty and the growth that comes from creating a plan initiated by God. He's ready to do something new in and through you! Are you ready to discover what that might be?

No makeover show or celebrity encounter could produce the kind of insight and growth your Creator can bring. I would encourage you to write down the seven steps

This truth is lived out when we see our insecurities becoming assets because the power of God Almighty is with us, shaping us with each step we take.

#MomEssentials

from the miracle we read in Mark and ask God to repeat those same actions in your own life. God is doing a new thing in each of us, and his glory will be evident when we allow others to be a part of our growth.

GOALS	PLANS	ACTIONS

CLOSING PRAYER

Lord, my human eyes and ears are overwhelmed with the world's noise and the activity of my own home. Help me to know more about you, to recognize your voice, and to follow your leading. You created me, and I know you have a beautiful purpose for my life. I don't want to stop growing, Lord; I want you to help me and teach me. May I have a teachable spirit, an open mind, and a heart that seeks only you. Shape me, Lord. Show me your ways, and I will walk in them. Amen.

6

MOM MOMENT

Matthew 19:26: "Jesus looked at them and said, 'With man this is impossible, but with God all things are possible.'"

DRIVER'S ED

Mom Essential: PERSPECTIVE

My foot pressed the accelerator to the floor as we sped across the four lanes of the main road in our small North Carolina town. Once through the intersection, I pulled over, checked my mirrors, and put the car in park. I looked to my right, expecting to see an approving smile from my examiner. Instead, I found a sweating, pale man. His right hand was securely gripping the door and his left was on the dash. His clipboard had fallen onto the floorboard, along with his glasses. My adrenaline was pumping, and I couldn't stop myself from letting out a small giggle.

My smile faded as the previously lovely instructor from the driver's license bureau turned into an angry, single-syllable-speaking sergeant. He yelled the word "out" through clenched teeth, but I didn't move. I was confused, and my face must have betrayed me. The man took a deep breath, picked up his clipboard, and put on his glasses. I asked what was wrong, and suddenly it was his turn to laugh as he filled me in:

"Didn't you see the traffic coming right at us?"

"I looked both ways. I thought we could make it, and you said 'go'!"

"I said 'no,' not 'go'!"

"Well, we made it, didn't we?"

"Get out. I'll be driving us back. Your test is finished."

I unbuckled, opened my door, and began walking around the car, hanging my head in shame. I was embarrassed, scared, and disappointed. The day had started out great and ended with my mother driving us home, my hand holding the tear-stained paper with the red letters *FAIL* stamped across it. My teenage hormones convinced my mind that life was over and I'd never be allowed to drive a car again.

It would be almost a year before I tried to take my driver's license test again. I was shaken by the fact that I had failed a test (which was unheard of in my life up to this point) and even worse, almost caused an accident. I simply couldn't understand how this happened. Before taking my driver's test, I attended classes, my parents worked with me, and I thought I was completely prepared. But, alas, I didn't see what my instructor was looking at, and I narrowly missed creating a dangerous situation for everyone. After taking more classes and practicing again with my parents, I finally earned the right to operate a motor vehicle. During the months between my attempts, I gained two important things: experience and perspective.

EXPERIENCE

Experience is a great word. In the sentence, "This is going to be an *experience* you'll never forget," it's a noun. But, it can turn into a verb when people say, "Just wait until you *experience* this." In the case of my first driving test, both definitions applied. No one could teach me how to drive by simply telling me about it; I had to get behind the wheel and do it myself. The more I experienced what it felt like to drive, what it required, and how to manage the situations around me, I started to gain confidence. With my newfound confidence, driving became an enjoyable experience.

Just as I had been ready to enjoy being a legal driver, I was even more determined to enjoy my first pregnancy. I attended every class our local hospital offered. I'd grown up babysitting other people's children and was even a nanny during my college years, but the idea of being responsible for my own child seemed a bit foreign to me. After sitting through the classes and watching the videos, I still had to experience the process of giving birth before any of the advice or options I'd been given applied to me. Becoming a mother is an event no one can outline for you, because for each woman, it is a unique experience. Thinking back on your journey through motherhood, what are some events you had to experience on your own before understanding what they entailed?

Take a moment to reflect on and remember some of the "firsts" you've encountered along the way:

I hope you were able to smile and laugh as you remembered moments when your eyes were opened and your life was forever changed. Once we've experienced something, the experience itself can never be taken away from us. When we encounter something on a personal level and interact with it in a fresh way, we can never go back and undo our experience. Life is made up of one experience leading to another, and if we continue to apply what we discover along the way, these experiences meld together to help us discover perspective.

PERSPECTIVE

When I was learning how to drive, my perspective was very technical. I left no room for unknown variables to occur. I was focused on myself and my process. By the time I took my second driver's test, I had a new perspective. It was one that took into account the other cars on the road and the uncertainty that comes when human beings are controlling fast-moving steel frames on wheels.

Each parenting experience in your list helped bring a new perspective into your life. Until you experienced a situation, you weren't able to have a true perspective concerning how it all would come together. Sharing these experiences with others allows each of us to walk away with our own unique perspective.

From potty training to cell phones, the issues we face will continually bring new challenges into our lives. When we reach out to someone who has experience in these areas, we begin to gain much-needed perspective. We might not want to emulate exactly what others have done, but we don't want to live in a vacuum or disregard the wisdom of others. In chapter 2, we wrote about our strength sources, and I'm certain some of those sources included the women in our lives. Along with helping us remain strong, they can also bring us a fresh and sometimes much-needed perspective.

The majority of the Proverbs were written by King David's son, Solomon. Solomon was wise and well spoken. His experience and perspective were filled with God's words. He wanted to make sure the wisdom God had shared with him was passed on to others, especially his descendants. Take a moment to read through the third chapter of Proverbs. As you read, keep track of how many times the words "wise" or "wisdom" are used, and write the total here: ________________.

Solomon personifies the word "wisdom" in verse 13, saying, "Blessed are those who find wisdom." There have been many moments in my life when I would have given anything to find wisdom as easily as I seemed to find folly.

What is wisdom? How will we know if we've found it, and how will it impact our daily lives? Using **Proverbs 3:13-35** as our guide, we can answer these questions and learn more about how wisdom can bring experience and perspective into our lives.

Someone who finds wisdom is ________________________ (v. 13).

Wisdom is more _____________________ than silver, returns better yields than _______________, and is more ___________________ than rubies (vv. 14-15).

The ways of wisdom are ____________________, and her paths are full of ________________ (v. 17).

We are not to let wisdom out of our _______________ (v. 21).

The wise inherit __________________ (v. 35).

In the past I would have pointed to someone advanced in age as being wise. I'm starting to rethink the necessity of age as a prerequisite to wisdom. Instead, I'm beginning to realize that experience plus perspective equals wisdom. Looking back to our Proverbs scripture, we see wisdom as more than just an understanding or mastery of a subject area. Wisdom is a beautiful gift because it brings us peace. Apply this equation to your life thus far. Write down an experience you've had, the perspective you acquired from it, and the wisdom you gained:

__________ + __________ = __________

experience perspective wisdom

At this point, we've studied five of our ten essentials. Take a moment to write down each essential in the list below (the first letter has been provided):

B ____________________

S ____________________

H ____________________

I ____________________

G ____________________

Which essential has challenged you the most thus far? __________________
If you had to choose an essential you have the most experience with, which one(s) would make the cut? __________________

Our sixth essential, perspective, allows us the opportunity to look back, look ahead, and honestly examine where we are on our journey. Perhaps some of the essentials within these pages seem completely out of reach for you, or haven't applied to your situation. If that's the case, please know it is okay. If we could master everything we read about, we'd be perfect. I'm fairly certain no one carrying the title of "mother" wants to add the burden of trying to be perfect all the time too! Whether you're a grandma or a new mom, you're experiencing a new season. Our perspective continues to change and grow. Each of us is currently being shaped into the woman God has called us to be, and God knows what we need. After reading **Matthew 6:25-34,** respond to the following statements:

List two items we are *not* to worry about.

____

______________________________ (v. 25)

Worry will *not* add what to our lives?

______________________________ (v. 27)

What items does our heavenly Father know we need?

______________________________ (vv. 31-32)

Should we worry about tomorrow? ________

Why or why not? ______________________

____

Each day I have with my children will bring enough trouble and worry without me bringing my own anxious thoughts and concerns to it. We are mothers forever. I would rather gain a right perspective now than wait until my children leave our home.

When we are focused on Jesus instead of our problems, we begin to see life through his eyes. With this new perspec-

Our sixth essential, perspective, allows us the opportunity to look back, look ahead, and honestly examine where we are on our journey.

tive, we find ourselves free from the pressure to be the one responsible for all things at all times. Even when things seem impossible, our perspective reminds us that we aren't alone and we don't have to be afraid. Referring to this chapter's Mom Moment, complete the message we read in Matthew 19:26:

"With __________ this is __________________________, but with

__________ all things are _______________________."

Many of us have heard about, or experienced firsthand, an issue that seemed impossible. Perhaps a medical diagnosis or a financial hardship came crashing down on us. Have you dealt with something that seemed impossible? Are you struggling with an "impossible" right now? As far as you are comfortable, use the space provided to write down as many details as you can about the impossible situation you are or were up against.

Perhaps this is the first time you've applied pen and paper to your "impossible" situation. Your willingness to try something new is admirable and shows you have a teachable spirit. Both these have a positive influence on your perspective. By writing things down, or even speaking them aloud, we recognize what we are facing and allow ourselves the freedom to surrender everything to the Lord, trust him to guide us, and gain a new perspective each step along the way.

Some of the greatest experiences and perspective-building opportunities come when we're faced with something impossible. Many of us have watched a seemingly impossible situation become possible. Take a moment to write down a time when God's faithful hand made a difference in your life or in someone else's life. Begin by naming the impossible and then explain how things changed so it became possible.

The Impossible

____

How It Became Possible

____

____

____

When we're against seemingly impossible situations, it's tempting to feel as though we are alone. But if all-powerful God is a part of our perspective, we find peace in recognizing that he is in control and will never leave us. Our Father in heaven loves us and has a beautiful plan for our lives (**Jeremiah 29:11**).

According to **Luke 8:22-25**, what question does Jesus ask his followers? (v. 25) ______________________________

____

When it comes to believing in God, believing his promises, and trusting him to help you through tough times, where is your faith? Would you rate your faith as weak, growing, or strong? In the chart on the next page, place an "x" next to the word that best represents your faith and ability to trust God with situations that seem impossible. Next, describe why you chose this word and what brought you to this point.

Where my faith is	Why it's this way
____ Weak ____ Growing ____ Strong	

A mother implementing the essential of perspective (along with the five essentials we previously studied) is a woman whose faith is unshaken. She can live this kind of life because she believes God cannot be shaken and his love will never fail. Fill in the missing words from the promise God gave to the prophet Isaiah:

"'Though the ____________________ be shaken and the hills be ____________________, yet my ______________________ __________ for you will not be shaken nor my covenant of _________________ be removed,' says the LORD, who has compassion on you" (Isaiah 54:10).

When a catastrophe hits and evil claws its way into innocent lives, we can look beyond the chaos and allow God's promises to shape our perspective. When the world around us stops making sense, we look to the One who created the heavens and earth. Our faith must remain strong and active whether we're living in chaos or in peace.

Earlier in this chapter, I referred to people advanced in age as being the ones we might label as being wise. These same people typically have a great perspective on life. This perspective is in place because they've had time to look back and see how situations were resolved, which relationships truly mattered, and what personal beliefs were most important. Ask a mother of multiple children what has changed since having only one child, and she'll list everything from the type of diapers she buys to her reuse of a pacifier that has fallen on the floor. Like experience, perspective can't be given; it has to be earned.

We've all gained perspective through our experiences. Some of us have more experiences than others, and the road we've taken has included different detours, bumps, and U-turns along the way. Right now, we're each going to create a road map of our lives. You'll find a completely blank page waiting for you to fill it with the road you've traveled. You choose the starting point, but this road should end with where you are right now in your life.

Here are some ideas to help you get started:

- *Possible starting points:* When you accepted Christ into your heart, when you found out you were pregnant, when you were married, when you graduated from school, when your children left for college, and so on.
- *Possible elements to help illustrate your journey:* Use signs such as stop, U-turn, bump, and so forth, to represent situations you faced. Draw pictures of buildings or people standing alongside the road. Make your road dip down or incline sharply to represent moments when you were on a mountaintop or in the valley.
- *Possible formats of your map:* A bird's-eye view, a list of directions such as you'd see on the map application on your phone, arrows, an actual road, and so forth.

There are endless possibilities—none either wrong or right. This is a map of your life thus far. Make it as detailed as you'd like. Fill the entire page with drawings, labels, or anything that helps illustrate your journey. No matter what you use, make this project about you and complete it your way! You are beautiful, unique women with an incredible story to tell. If you're participating in this study with a group of women, I'd encourage you to have a time

> *Our faith must remain strong and active whether we're living in chaos or in peace.*
> #MomEssentials

MY ROAD MAP SO FAR

when everyone who would like to can share her map and tell her story; I guarantee you'll learn something new. Have fun with this project. The finished product is your testimony, your story—make it your own and revel in how far you've come!

The first time I drove my car at night, I was tense and nervous. We were on a country road with no streetlights to help me see what lay ahead. My dad sensed my anxiety level rising. He reminded me that I only needed to worry about what was illuminated by the headlights. Dad suggested I focus on what I could see instead of worrying about what I couldn't.

What a beautiful illustration of our equation: experience + perspective = wisdom. Our **experiences** occur in real time, and some situations come out of nowhere (like driving along a dark road). Our **perspective** comes from what we can see and the information directly at our disposal within the moment (the amount of road shown by the headlights). **Wisdom** is gained as we begin to enjoy the ride, gain new maneuvers to deal with hazards, and begin to react appropriately to any unforeseen detours. The road map you created for your life is full of experiences. These experiences have worked together to influence your perspective about faith, family, love, and all aspects of life. Wisdom comes when we take time to look back on our lives and realize how God's hand was moving in our circumstances.

God's plan for our lives is not defined by our perspective. Let me say that another way: our perspective doesn't dictate or limit God's plan for our lives. Isn't that a wonderful promise? God doesn't plan or prepare as we do. He is Lord of heaven and earth, and yet he knows each hair on our head (**Luke 12:7**) and no detail escapes his attention. We can trust God with our lives, and we can trust him to guide us through our day. We can ask God to help us see our impossible or difficult situation through *his* eyes. Because we live in a fallen world, our road will be filled with ups, downs, and moments in between. No matter what you are facing, you have God on your side, and I'm certain your friends and family would like to join you on this journey as well.

If you are new to the Christian life and this talk of faith, hope, and trust seems a bit foreign to you, please take heart. Jesus came to earth to show us how real God's love and presence can be in our lives. Read **John 3:16-17** and complete the verses:

"For God so _____________ the world that he gave his one and only

Son, that whoever _______________ in him shall not perish but have eternal __________. For God did not send

his Son into the world to ______________

the world, but to ____________ the world

through him."

His Spirit brings us comfort and his Scriptures bring us focus. #MomEssentials

I could never imagine sacrificing my child so other people could have the opportunity to experience God's love and peace. Yet that's exactly what God did. He wants to save us and save the world. You'd think the people closest to Jesus, his disciples, would have been the first to hear and understand this message. Yet after years of walking along the road with Jesus, seeing firsthand how Jesus did the impossible (healing the blind, raising the dead, calming a storm, and so forth), some of the disciples *still* didn't recognize Jesus as God's Son. Because Jesus' ministry was coming to an end and he was preparing to die on the cross, Jesus began speaking in clear, specific terms with his followers. When the disciples finally realized Jesus was God's Son, they were also being prepared to say good-bye to him. Read **John 16:28-33** to fully understand the dialogue between Jesus and the disciples.

According to these verses, the disciples gained a new perspective. They were able to "see" Jesus in a new light; they now saw him as coming from God. Jesus' words in verse 33 also bring a new perspective to our lives. He tells us that we *will* have trouble in this life, but he desires for us to have peace. I interpret this to mean that even when I'm faced with something that seems impossible, I have a God who will bring me peace and perspective. Write the last sentence from **John 16:33** below:

____

____

Take heart, my sister in Christ, Jesus has overcome this world, and he will help us overcome whatever situation we're facing. Our perspective should be the same as Christ when he said in **John 16:32**, "Yet I am not alone, for my Father is with me."

When I think back to my first attempt to pass the driver's license test, I begin to wonder what thoughts were running through my instructor's mind as I crossed four lanes of traffic at the wrong time. His perspective was different from mine. He saw the impending danger and tried to warn me, but I charged ahead anyway. When issues come up and we can't see past the immediate situation, we have to stop and remember that God is with us. His Spirit brings us comfort and his Scriptures bring us focus. We can begin putting our faith in action once we understand that our perspective isn't the only one that exists or matters.

CLOSING PRAYER

Thank you, Lord, for bringing me this far on my journey. I recognize that without your guiding hand and faithful presence, the road I traveled could have been much more difficult. I need your presence today, Lord. You accept me just as I am, and I know I can be honest with you, so today I'd like to give you my impossible situations. I want to put my faith in action and take your perspective as my own. I trust you, Lord. I give you my day and everything that will happen in the next twenty-four hours. Help me apply the essentials I've studied so far. Please help my perspective stay focused on what and who matters most. Amen.

7

CAN YOU HOLD, PLEASE?

Mom Essential: DISCIPLINE

MOM MOMENT

Ecclesiastes 3:1: "There is a time for everything, and a season for every activity under the heavens."

Chocolate.
Facebook.
Retail sales.
Email.

These are just *some* of the items and activities that fight for my attention. I can sit down to "quickly" check things on my computer and the next thing I know, an hour has passed. My intention to just "look around" becomes an afternoon of justification and purchases. How can such wonderful items have a negative impact on my day? It happens when I lack discipline and the benefits in my life turn into burdens.

When we apply the essential of discipline, we are preparing our hearts to apply all of the themes we're studying (put together, shaped up, equipped). The ability to be disciplined and control our personal impulses helps us to fulfill our responsibilities as mothers. Some examples of discipline could include things like not having dessert with every meal, not looking at the phone each time it buzzes with an alert, or even the simple act of getting up a little earlier than our children.

Allowing God to shape my life requires that I have discipline. This means I control a behavior because of the training I've received. Even with training, there are some behaviors I struggle to control. When this happens, I make a plan and make a choice to be disciplined, even when it's difficult. When I practice discipline, I am making a statement about how much I value my life and my role as a mom. Without discipline, I begin to lose myself in the events and demands that fill my day.

As we begin our discussion concerning discipline in our lives, take a moment to list any substances, activities, or other items that begin as positive but have the potential to overtake people's lives:

____

____

____

The essential of discipline is easier to apply when an activity isn't enjoyable. However, if something brings pleasure (or distraction) it can consume time and energy very quickly. Discover what **Proverbs 25:28** says about a form of discipline called self-control:

"Like a city whose ____________ are ___________________ through is a person who ____________ self-control."

There have been moments in my life when I've put up walls to protect myself. I created them to try to keep people out of my life. Thankfully, I had friends who broke through those walls and rescued me. The walls mentioned in the verse from Proverbs are walls intended to ensure the protection and survival of the inhabitants within their shadow.

We try to keep our children safe, and that's important. From warnings about running with scissors, to explaining why they can't eat food they find on the ground, we are always trying to keep our children and family protected. Harm can come from outside our house, and sometimes it can come from within. It's never intentional, but danger can sneak into our home due to a lack of discipline. Can you think of any habits or behaviors that have broken through the protective walls around your family and are creating havoc? All of us can answer yes. Some issues might be more severe than others, but everyone struggles at some point with how to live in the world without the world controlling our lives.

Satan is a smart, cunning, sly enemy. He's like the strangers we warn our kids about. Satan will offer us something that sounds and feels great. It might even satisfy

"'I have the right to do anything,' you say—but not everything is beneficial. 'I have the right to do anything'—but not everything is constructive."
—1 Corinthians 10:23

us for a time, but this sweet temptation hides a long road full of denial, fear, and perhaps destruction. Like a tiny crack in a wall, these behaviors start small. As mothers it's important we know what signs to look for along the way. When we are disciplined and practice self-control, we're able to interpret and perceive impending danger.

When my grandmother was raising her family, she was dealing with the influence of rock-n-roll and the Beatles. These might seem like trivial concerns to us, but they were legitimate issues to her generation. Our society and ethical climate are constantly changing. The issues we face are new and sometimes very difficult to sort through. One item I've begun to take to task is a little thing called "technology." Before anyone starts throwing their smartphones away, I want to look at how technology has impacted our society and, in turn, our family.

We don't go out to eat on a regular basis, but I love having dinner with all my guys. It's a wonderful thing when someone else is preparing the food and washing the dishes. When we do go out, I've started looking around the restaurant and counting how many families are sitting at their table, talking to each other. I know it sounds basic and perhaps assumed, but you'd be surprised how difficult it is to find adults and children engaged in conversation while sharing a meal. Instead I find members of a family sitting at the same table with each person looking down at their personal device, lost in a world they control and enjoy. Before I begin sounding like my almost one-hundred-year-old grandpa, reminiscing about the "good ol'" days, please know I love technology and all that it has done for our world. But some of the extras we utilize have disguised themselves as essentials. You see, technology isn't bad, but it can become bloated if it isn't kept in check with what is best for our family. How can we apply the concept of **1 Corinthians 10:23** to the issue of technology?

____

____

____

Technology is all around us, and without it, we wouldn't be able to communicate with others, record our memories, or in some cases, complete our work. However, when we don't set boundaries or limits to the things of this world, we willingly surrender to their power. Soon, they begin to break down the walls of safety and protection we've placed around our family. Sometimes I feel as though I'm fighting against technology, and this battle does not have clearly defined boundaries or sides.

Along with my desire to be disciplined in my use of technology, I need to remember what kind of weapons and battle plans I have at my disposal. **Second Corinthians 10:4-5** sounds more like a battle cry than a Sunday school lesson, but these words remind us why it's so important to be disciplined, alert, and aware of the enemy's tactics.

> "The _______________ we fight with are not the weapons of the world. On the contrary, they have divine power to _______________ _____________________. We demolish ___________________ and every ________________________ that sets itself up against the knowledge of God, and we ___________ ____________________ every thought to make it obedient to Christ."

I consider myself to be a strong woman, but I would never claim to be able to demolish strongholds or arguments. I have to rely on God's weapons—weapons that are not of this world—in order to live a disciplined life. I want a life that is free of strongholds, arguments, and pretensions. But I live on earth, so I know these will always exist. Let's discover how to demolish strongholds and arguments and what kinds of weapons we'll need to be successful. Put on your battle gear and get ready to dig a trench. We are fighting for our families, and we won't allow Satan to win. Instead,

The day technology has more time with my child than I do is the day I've relinquished my influence and impact on my child's life.
#MomEssentials

we're going to have the discipline to be obedient to Christ and arm ourselves with knowledge from Scripture and the divine power of the Holy Spirit.

STRONGHOLDS

A stronghold is defined as a place that is fortified, something that can easily be defended and is difficult to tear down. Technology can become a stronghold when it creates barriers between people. Unfortunately, some of us have remained blissfully ignorant as the world around us embraces the latest gaming systems, tablets, and Internet sites. As a result, many of us don't understand the kinds of temptations and exposure available to our children through the devices they use. Many websites and computer programs are available to help us limit the cyber-predator or inappropriate video trying to pop up on our child's screen. Those are weapons of this world. When we look back to our scripture from 2 Corinthians, we're reminded that our weapons are "not the weapons of the world." We have access to some amazing, supernaturally powered weapons. The only question is, do we have the discipline and guts to apply them?

No one enjoys being the "bad guy," but we have to be stronger than the power of the devices in our home. From our television to the gaming system, all of it has to remain under our disciplined eye. The day technology has more time with my child than I do is the day I've relinquished my influence and impact on my child's life. We have to be disciplined enough to see this happening and put a stop to it. In case we need even more encouragement to take a stand, let's look at 2 Timothy 1:7:

"For the Spirit God gave us does not make us ____________, but gives us ____________, love and ______________________."

The Spirit God has given us calls us to exercise our power, love, and self-discipline, especially when it comes to our family. So don't be afraid to limit the amount of screen time your children have. There are times when technology saves our sanity (long waits at the DMV, doctor's office, road trips, and so on), and there are other times when it becomes a substitute. If you're wondering where to start, I'd encourage you to think about mealtimes. Many of us are running to practices, work, and rehearsals, so our time around a table is limited. To me, this makes mealtimes even more of a priority. When we are finally able to sit down and be together, we should be communicating with each other, face-to-face with our voices.

From the beginning of time, God meant for us to communicate with each other. The Bible tells us that God talked with Adam and Eve in the garden of Eden, and he didn't want the conversation to stop simply because sin entered the world (Genesis 3). In Deuteronomy 6, the Israelites were instructed to share God's truth with their children. After reading **Deuteronomy 6:4-9**, answer the following questions:

How can we ensure that technology will help us continue to love God with all our heart, soul, and strength?

____

____

____

When we limit the amount of screen time our children have, we increase the amount of time they can spend with us and the energy they will need from us. How can you be disciplined with your own time and technology to make sure you're prepared to interact with and enjoy your children when they ask for your attention?

____

____

____

One of the toughest moments in my mothering career was the day I asked my son a question and he answered me while keeping his eyes glued to his personal device. I became angry and asked how he could dare disrespect me. I gave him a lecture about looking people in the eye when listening to and responding to them. I thought I was acting in righteous anger but found myself humbled and keenly aware of my own downfalls when he told me that I often answer his questions and talk to him without looking up from my phone. Ouch! I'd unknowingly taught my son that what I was doing on my phone or computer was just as important as his question or his need. I apologized, and that night we all talked about some rules in our house when it comes to technology.

Do you have rules in your house to keep technology from establishing a negative stronghold within your family's relationships?

____

____

____

I'm not preaching against technology. I'm making a stand against technology being allowed to form a stronghold in our home and the relationships within our family. Practicing discipline is tough, but we need to remember that the spirit we have is one of self-control and power; we don't have to be timid. Let's mute our phones, look at our children when they call our name, and refuse to check a status update in the middle of a meal. All of it can wait; our families shouldn't have to wait. Time passes so quickly. It's easy to remain unaware of how much time we spend with technology. I would challenge all of us to keep a running tab of how many minutes we spend looking, listening, and interacting with the technical items in our lives. This is meant to bring awareness. Through this awareness, we can become disciplined in how and when we allow technology into our lives.

ARGUMENTS

I hope I'm not the only one that has fallen victim to using technology as my soapbox. Too many times I've written an email or posted a status that was from a place of selfish desires and vain conceit. Complete this challenging scripture from **Philippians 2:3-4**:

"Do ____________________ out of selfish ambition or vain

________________. Rather, in ________________ value others

above yourselves, not looking to your ________ interests but each

of you to the ____________________ of the others."

A verbal argument is tough to endure, but it can become even more difficult to resolve when technology gets in the way. When our ambitions are focused on others, we are more apt to think about how that person feels. This disciplined mind-set encourages us to protect the other person instead of attacking him or her while enjoying the safety and distance our screen provides.

Have you experienced a time when someone attacked you while communicating through technology? Did you respond in person, give the person a call, or use the same avenue to retaliate? I wonder if we could avoid some misinterpretations or hurt feelings if we took time to find people and express our concerns face-to-face.

Think of a time when a message delivered by technology started an argument within your spirit or with someone else. Perhaps it was a political statement or a direct insult to someone you love. Write about how technology exacerbates or eliminates these types of arguments, through outlets such as Twitter, Facebook, email, and so on.

Depending on the ages of our children, we'll see technology in a new and different light. No one can tell us exactly how to manage technology, but I want to make sure it is never managing me or dictating the activities in my family's life. Having the discipline to keep technology in its place is almost a full-time job. But we are strong and able to take on this task because we are in shape, and we've been put together by God himself! Even though today's inventions are revolutionary, Scripture assures us that the temptations technology might bring aren't new at all.

First Corinthians 10:13 tells us how to respond when a stronghold or argument comes our way and shows us that we aren't alone in our struggles. God is faithful to help us, and we will be able to endure! Please fill in the missing words from this wonderful New Testament passage:

> "No temptation has _______________ you except what is
>
> _______________ to mankind. And God is ___________________;
>
> he will not let you be tempted beyond what you can _____________.
>
> But when you are tempted, he will also provide a _______
>
> ________________ so that you can endure it."

A temptation can take on different forms. Scripture warns us not to project our own issues onto others because everyone is unique. One person might struggle with overspending and therefore avoids unnecessary trips to the shopping mall. Does this mean the shopping mall is a bad place? Not necessarily, but it is a source of temptation for certain people. Whether it's a substance or an action, we all lack discipline in one area or another. The words of 1 Corinthians—"common to mankind"—are meant to reassure and reaffirm the idea that we are all dealing with what it means to live in a sin-filled world.

Let's apply the first sentence from verse 13—"No temptation has overtaken you except what is common to mankind"—to our areas of discussion: strongholds and arguments. For the purpose of study and application, let's replace the word "temptation" in this verse with the words "stronghold" and "argument." As you respond to the following questions and prompts, I pray the Holy Spirit will guide your thoughts and reveal God's love to you no matter what you are facing. Be honest and be real.

Allow God to reshape your own desire for discipline in your life and the life of your family.

No stronghold has overtaken you except what is common to mankind.

Some strongholds technology has created in our home include. . .

____

____

I'm fighting against these strongholds by . . .

____

____

God has shown his faithfulness during this time through . . .

____

____

No argument has overtaken you except what is common to mankind.

An argument I keep dealing with involves . . .

____

____

If technology is the source of the argument, I can make a plan to . . .

____

____

God has shown his faithfulness during this time through . . .

____

____

Have you ever called a company and the operator immediately asked you to hold? I've never had the guts to say "no" to this request, but I really don't like complying. I never want to ask my children to sit on hold while I complete an activity that is motivated or completed by technology. There are times when I'm working and I am required to spend time with my computer. During these moments, the technology I'm using has specific start and stop times, so my children don't have to compete for my attention all day long. When I'm working, I'm required to complete certain activities. When I'm not working I want to be 100 percent their mom and not distracted by the buzzing, beeping devices surrounding me.

Let's become mothers who model for our children what it means to put others first and be disciplined when it comes to our use of technology. We want to make technology work for us, not the other way around. As we finish our theme, Shaped Up, I want to focus on a beautiful scripture from **Ephesians 4:22-24**. As we move forward with our plans, we'll learn even more about ourselves and our Savior. God is making us into something new, and it's a beautiful process.

> "You were taught, with regard to your former way of life, to
>
> _______ _______ your old self, which is being corrupted by its
>
> deceitful desires; to be __________ ________ in the attitude of your
>
> ___________; and to put on the ________ ___________, created to
>
> be like God in true righteousness and holiness."

Our "new self" can help us be disciplined and follow through with our plan. Our plan will bring a new perspective concerning technology. Some families discipline their children by having them sit in time-out. What if we put our technology there too? I like the sound of a "technology time-out." At first it will seem difficult, but we can retrain and "put off" our old self in order to enjoy the new perspective God has waiting for us. Take a moment to read the Mom Moment located at the beginning of this chapter. There is a time and place for technology. Let's practice the discipline of keeping it from monopolizing our time and our thoughts. Our children need us more than we need technology.

CLOSING PRAYER

Lord, you know the intentions of my heart would never be to put technology above my children. Please show me if this has happened and how to be strong in my response and reaction to this issue. Strengthen my spirit, Lord, as I face a world that relies on technology more than you. Keep me focused on your voice and alert to your nudges. Please shape our family and our time so that we truly seek after you and love you with all our hearts, minds, and souls. Amen.

THEME 3

EQUIPPED

8

AN ATTITUDE OF ACTION

Mom Essential: PREPARATION

MOM MOMENT

Galatians 6:7*b*:

"A man reaps what he sows."

I remember watching my toddler son stand precariously on a small plastic chair, stretching his chubby little arm toward the countertop. All he wanted was the bright red tail of his airplane, and he was sure he could reach it. My first response was to intercept his attempt and get the plane for him, but something stopped me. I watched as he was almost there, and whoosh! His chair slipped out from under him. Suddenly the airplane, my son, and his pride were splattered on the kitchen floor.

I ran to him and scooped him up. With compassion in my voice I said, "Uh-oh, baby fall. So sad. So sad. . . ." Once his tears subsided, I put the plane back on top of the counter, set his chair upright, and looked him in the eye. I pointed to the plane, "Plane? Plane?" He nodded his head yes, his eyes wide with expectation.

At the time, my husband and I were teaching him to use baby sign language. We used signing as a tool to help our kids, but we kept things pretty basic. Our boys learned words like eat, more, please, all done, and the most important sign: help.

Sitting in front of him on the floor, I made the sign for "help" and molded his chubby hands to make the same sign and action. Once he made the sign on his own, I quickly reached for the plane and placed it in his lap.

We practiced this same modeling and response a couple times with the plane going on the counter and then into his lap. The key was that he only received the plane once he'd made the sign for help. In that moment I was trying to teach my son that he *can* help himself and accomplish lots of things on his own. If something becomes too tough and he can't do it alone, he simply needs to ask for help.

Take a moment to compare this story with our challenge from **Galatians 6:7** (our Mom Moment for this chapter).

What was I "sowing" into my little boy's mind and heart?

____

____

____

____

Assuming this teaching moment will make a lasting impression, what will I reap as a result of my efforts?

____

____

____

____

If you have multiple children, the thought of taking time to teach one child one lesson might seem impossible or like a waste of time. But wouldn't we rather teach our children lessons now, when the repercussions are fairly short-lived and small, than when they are teenagers and the world brings serious consequences to their lives? When these kinds of overwhelming or negative thoughts enter our minds, we need to speak a word of truth (**Ephesians 4:15**) and extinguish any doubts or excuses from the enemy.

Scripture warns us against an enemy that comes against us with one goal in mind: to steal, kill, and destroy (**John 10:10**). Satan is on the prowl, and we are the guardians sent to protect our family!

As mothers we don't have the option of giving up, giving in, or giving out. We are called to be strong, to set goals, and to be prepared! We know some moments might be rough, but we will not give up because nothing involved with being a mom is easy.

NOTES

Whether it's holding strong to the expectations we've set for our children's behavior or conquering a health goal, we cannot give up; our family is counting on us. Galatians 6:9 says it best:

> "Let us not ____________ ___________ in
>
> doing good, for at the proper time we will
>
> __________ ____ ______________ if we
>
> ______ ________ ___________ ______."

When you look at your family and your life, what kind of harvest are you working toward? What kind of adults would you like your children to become? These might seem like easy questions, but the answers can be difficult to apply. Sometimes our reality doesn't match the expectations we have. Talk to parents whose children have chosen to walk away from their faith or their family. The hurt that comes with this kind of reality brings a choice. Parents can give up or they can choose to act.

When disappointment occurs, we turn to Scripture and to the leading of the Holy Spirit to tell us which direction to go and how to move forward wisely. Sometimes all we can do is pray and leave our children in the hands of their Creator. Sometimes action is necessary. We will know how to prepare and respond when we see things from God's perspective. Each of us has unique gifts and talents to apply when we parent. The most important attribute is the tenacity to keep going. No matter the situation, we believe God has given us everything we need to be successful, and someday, at some point we will see the fruit of our labor.

While Jesus was on earth, he labored and toiled without seeing much return on his investment, at least in the eyes of the world. But being the wise, loving Savior he is,

Jesus knew the world would soon understand his message of love, grace, and peace. One of the ways Jesus reached different groups of people was through telling stories. These stories are called parables, and they always had a hidden, deeper meaning behind their story line. His intentions were to connect with and better teach the people who were listening to him.

The parable of the talents is a story of three servants who were trusted with physical coins called talents. Read **Matthew 25:14-30** and discover how each man responded to his responsibilities. As you read, fill in the details of this parable.

Servant No. 1 was given _____ talents and gained ______ more.

Total talents = _______.

Servant No. 2 was given _____ talents and gained ______ more.

Total talents = _______.

Servant No. 3 was given _____ talents and gained ______ more.

Total talents = _______.

In verse 14, Jesus introduces the characters of our tale: a man getting ready to leave on a journey (the master) and three of his servants. Verse 15 says the man chose the amount of talents to give each servant according to his ______________.

We can determine the master knew his servants well and had seen their abilities in action. He knew the kind of training, experience, and work ethic each man possessed. Even the third servant, who obviously wasn't extremely successful, received something. He wasn't overlooked because he didn't come with the same level of abilities as the other servants; instead, he was given the same opportunity as the other two men.

God has given each of us specific abilities. Some of us are amazing at keeping things organized. Others can make a meal without glancing at a cookbook. Our abilities might differ, but one thing is certain; each of us is prepared to care for our family.

Take a moment to write down some of your characteristics and tasks you feel you do well. It's okay to brag on yourself a bit. Think about how, when, and where you see those abilities being used and write about them in the space provided.

MAGNIFICENT!

SUPER!

FANTASTIC!

FABULOUS!

GREAT!

If you had a difficult time coming up with some abilities of your own, perhaps you could ask your husband, friends, or children. Even if it doesn't seem like it, they are always watching and noticing what you do. We can have confidence in God's design and remember that God is equipping us each day so we can become a perfectly prepared mom for our family.

When the master in our story gave coins (or talents) to the three servants, he didn't give them specific instructions; he only provided them with a starting point (five, two, and one talent respectively). Through Jesus' parable, we can gain an understanding of how God sees our changing role as a mom and how he expects us to respond. We aren't told exactly what to do with things like crafts, housekeeping, volunteer work, and so on. Instead, we're given children, Scripture, and prayer. The strengths we possess will be revealed as we do what we think is best for our family.

Verses 21 and 23 of our parable record the master's response to the first two servants. Write down what the master said to them:

____

____

____

Part of raising a family is the daunting task of helping our children prepare for the next transition in their lives. Whether it's preschool or college, we need to look ahead in our child's life and know what actions need to happen now to help him or her in the future. Although my role of mom will never be over, it will change. My prayer is that no matter what choices my children make for themselves, I will be able to hear my heavenly Father greet me at heaven's gates with the same phrase you wrote down: "Well done, good and faithful servant!"

When we are able to start small and do well with what we've been given, our Master knows we can handle more. The old saying "God never gives you more than you can handle" is true, but I'd like to create our own saying for these days of parenting and transitions: "You can handle whatever life brings because God has put you together, shaped you, and equipped you for this moment."

Sometimes we have to endure difficult times or even repetition before we discover how wonderful our abilities really are. God has prepared us for the moments when we need to decide on what actions to take, whether that means cleaning a room or helping a child through a life transition. Discover this promise in **2 Peter 1:3**:

> "His divine ________________ has given us everything we need
>
> for a godly life through our ______________________ of him who
>
> _______________ us by his own glory and goodness."

Did you catch that last phrase? You have been *called*. Do you believe God has called you to this place and position? I do. I believe God knows exactly how much strength to apportion my way. I can trust his leading and believe in the abilities God has given me to fulfill my calling in life. Caring for our children throughout various stages might prove to be a challenge. But if we believe God has given us everything we need and prepared us for each season, our confidence and commitment to this journey won't waver.

When we doubt our abilities and gifts, we essentially doubt God and open ourselves up to becoming like the third servant in our story. He lived in fear and never took action. In turn he was called "lazy and wicked" (v. 26). We aren't required to be perfect, but we are required to give our best and *try*. I don't want to end up like the third servant, choosing to live in fear of trying something new. I want to move forward with confidence, knowing God has equipped me for the tasks ahead.

You drew a map in chapter 6 outlining the journey you've taken up to the point of becoming a mother. The essential in chapter 6 was perspective, and I think it's much easier to have a healthy perspective on things when we can look back over them. It's much more challenging to keep a proper perspective when looking ahead to the unknown. However, if we apply the truths from this chapter's scriptures, we will realize we are prepared and claim God's equipping presence while moving forward with our goals and plans.

Before we draw the rest of our map, we need to be reminded of an important message from **Isaiah 55:8**. We looked at this verse in chapter 1. Just for fun, see if you can fill in the missing words:

"'For my ________________ are not your thoughts, neither are your ___________ my ways,' declares the LORD."

We would never claim to know what God has planned or predict what will happen in our lives. We aren't fortune-tellers, but we are women with sharp minds and sensitive spirits. Take a moment and reflect on the essentials we've covered. I would encourage you to look back through this study and find any scriptures you circled, highlighted, or remember as having an impact on you.

thoughts / important quotes / scriptures

After spending time in prayer and reflection, we're ready to look ahead to the future. Using the space provided, please create a map that begins with today. Your map can end at any point, but remember: this map is about you and you alone. Perhaps you've wanted to go back to school or try a new career path. Write down where you want to be and when you think it might be possible to make that dream a reality.

After creating a map for your action items, go back through your map and add in any major events that are certain to happen in your family's life (graduations, birthdays, and so on). Seeing how these events line up with your goals helps you grasp the timeline we are dealing with. You are recording ideas, hopes, dreams, and goals. We write these things down while keeping the truth from Isaiah 55 in the forefront of our mind. Thank you for making this project your own. I hope you enjoy this time of dreaming and planning. (See page 120.)

Our Mom Moment clearly states that our current actions and reactions have consequences in the future. Even when we make a mistake or something doesn't work out as we'd hoped, we know that God is still in control. If God has truly put us together and shaped our lives into his creation, we've discovered what it means to trust him completely. When our faith is secure, our hope is strong and we can feel prepared to respond correctly to any situation that comes our way.

What are you sowing today to help you and your family move toward the goals you've recorded on your map? We don't need to have all the answers right now, but we want to start preparing for the way ahead. Thinking ahead can help us avoid feeling overwhelmed with our present situation. Everything is working together for God's great purpose (**Romans 8:28**). God allows us to experience

NOTES

MY ROAD MAP FOR THE FUTURE

whatever happens today so we'll be better equipped for the future. Allow him to equip and prepare you for the wonderful things he has in store for your life!

CLOSING PRAYER

Thank you, Lord, for giving me the specific abilities I need to help our family navigate this crazy time of life. Lord, I know you have wonderful plans for each member of my family and for me. Help me to remember that you are going to use everything that happens today to prepare me and my family for what is coming in our future. Help me not to become weary from doing this good work. Bring me your peace and help me to hear your voice as I prepare to invest in my family and in myself. Give me wisdom to know what actions to take and when to take them. You are a faithful God, and for that I praise your name! Amen.

9

HELP WANTED

Mom Essential: NETWORKING

MOM MOMENT

Romans 12:10*a*: "Be devoted to one another in love."

The old saying, "It takes a village," typically refers to raising children. I think mothers also need a community of women, or a village, raising them. I have accepted the idea that I will never be able to know all things at all times. I've also silenced the stubborn voice in my head telling me I can survive and succeed on my own. We began this study with the understanding that reading Scripture and having an active prayer life should be essentials in our lives. These actions help us connect with God. The devotion God has toward us, his creation, is amazing. He was willing to sacrifice his only Son so we could enjoy eternal life. But God isn't concerned merely with our eternal salvation; he wants to make sure our daily needs are met as well. God sends his Spirit to be with us each and every day. God's "Spirit of truth," or Holy Spirit, acts as a helper and comforter and is available to us at all times. (See **John 14:17**.)

Connecting with our Creator through Scripture and prayer are important, but so are the relationships we have here on earth. Throughout this study, we've acknowledged the people in our lives and how much they impact us. When it comes to networking, we need to be intentional about surrounding ourselves with women who help us grow stronger in our faith. Ask anyone in a leadership role and they will support this universal truth: our associates have a direct effect on our outcomes. Who we associate with impacts who we are becoming. Whether you meet with a weekly playgroup or have a strong connection with women at your workplace or church, making yourself available to others (networking) is key to ensuring continued growth in your life.

In chapter 2, we reflected on tough events from the past and how we were able to make it through. I'm certain many of us had a list of strength sources that included the names of specific people. If your list contained people's names, I hope you've had the opportunity to let them know how they impacted your life. Telling someone thank you or sharing updates from your journey can encourage others and develop a connection that will last beyond your friendship here on earth. When we let people know how they have influenced us, we create a network of people who truly care about us and honestly know us. The purpose of having friends isn't only to have help when times get tough. We connect with other moms to help us remain grounded and encouraged in our daily life. The Lord can use anyone, even us, to bring strength and hope to others. We just have to be willing to network, connect, and be real with other women.

When Jesus left heaven, he came to earth to teach people about God's love and redemptive grace. He could have come to earth, preached the good news, healed people, and been celebrated all by himself. He didn't need human help, but he chose it. He decided to surround himself with people just like you and me. Jesus' associates and friends were human, flawed in all sorts of ways.

The Creator of heaven and earth decided to have a group of fishermen and tax collectors as his support group. If Christ chose to associate with his disciples during such a crucial time of his ministry and life, I think we should follow this example and seek a group of our own as well. They don't have to be a group of perfect people—just real women willing to be real friends to us and to our children.

NOTES

During his time on earth, Jesus showed us that God can use anyone. Jesus reached out and created a network of twelve men. He helped them connect with each other and to his cause. To help us think more about the people who we should network with and how they play a role in our lives, let's use Jesus' example from the New Testament book of Luke. Record the apostles' names below as you read **Luke 6:12-16**.

______________________	______________________
______________________	______________________
______________________	______________________
______________________	______________________
______________________	______________________
______________________	______________________

We discover two distinct names for this group of men in verse 13:

"When morning came, he called his ______________ to him and chose twelve of them, whom he also designated ______________."

I've heard many sermons preached and illustrations given concerning the fact that we don't have to be perfect before God can use us. Hearing these truths is one thing, but I love seeing them in a real-world scenario through Scripture. Studying this group of ragtag men provides a beautiful example of what can happen when God's hand is at work putting people together, shaping them for his purpose, and equipping them for his work. With these twelve men, God was going to change the world. But first, he had to change *them*.

Jesus had hundreds of people following him from town to town, but at the beginning of his ministry, Jesus called these twelve to leave everything behind, follow him, and learn from him. They were set apart and called away from the masses. When we become mothers, I believe God is calling us to something so special we sometimes have to leave the world and focus on learning about our new role from our heavenly Father. We don't leave behind who we were before we had children; we simply become something better and more beautiful as God begins to equip us for our calling.

To better understand how God was working with this group of men, we need to know the meaning behind two key words in this Scripture:

The word "disciples" is the Greek word *mathetes,* which means "learners, students."

The word "apostles" is the Greek word *apostoloi,* meaning "messengers, sent ones."

In his book *Twelve Ordinary Men,* John MacArthur takes an in-depth look at each disciple and the role he played in supporting Jesus' ministry and helping the church thrive. MacArthur helps us grasp the incredible responsibility and seemingly impossible timeline the disciples were up against during their time of transformation:

> These few men, whose backgrounds were in mundane trades and earthly occupations, had little more than eighteen months' training for the monumental task to which they were called. There was no second string, no backup players, no plan B if the Twelve should fail.[1]

As mothers there are times when we feel ill-prepared and completely overwhelmed. Sometimes I wish there were a "relief mommy" waiting in the wings just in case I don't have what it takes. We may not have another mom waiting to take our place, but we do have moms that can help us each step along the way.

Some of us are discovering what it means to be *mathetes.* We are active students of life, learning everything we can each day. Mothering and parenthood is tougher than any academic course I can think of, and so much is on the line! Like the disciples, we are responsible for learning everything we can and applying it to the best of our ability.

I hope I never stop learning and discovering new things—that's what makes life worth living! If I ever did figure it all out, I have to wonder if I'd just shrivel up with boredom. There are certain parts of life where I will always be a *mathetes* (disciple), continuing to learn more. One day my children will start driving, go to college, marry, and if the Lord desires, have children of their own. I've never been a mother of three boys these ages before. I've never been fortysomething before. Every year things change and the understanding that I'm going to learn something new becomes a bit more comfortable.

Take a moment to read **Ecclesiastes 3:1-8**. In the space provided, write down which of these "times" is the most difficult for you to endure. Next to each, record how the women in your "village" have helped or could help you. An example has been given from my own personal chart.

Time (Event)	Help from my network of believers
"a time to refrain from embracing"	*I struggle with the idea of letting my kids go. Whether it's college or marriage, I know I'm going to find it difficult. I could ask mothers who are older than me how they coped and what helped them let go.*

Being a disciple can become overwhelming and exhausting if we stay in the learning phase of life for too long. I enjoy seeing my time of learning grow into a time of confidence and understanding. One time this happened for me was after the birth of our first son. Although it isn't for everyone, I had decided to breastfeed. I remember becoming frustrated with myself and my son. Things weren't going well, but the nurses kept encouraging me. They assured me that someday feeding times would be easy and enjoyable. In my *mathetes* state of mind I was getting tired of trying and failing. My personal goal, to breastfeed my son, was still in front of me, and I decided not to give up.

I'm happy to report that my efforts paid off. By the time my third child was born I could have him latched on while simultaneously putting a puzzle together with my toddler and talking on the phone. I became an *apostole* of breastfeeding. I was aware of the lessons I'd learned and what the experience had taught me. I was now an apostle and had discovered some truths I could share with others.

The best part about being a parent is that each phase of life brings a chance to be both a disciple and an apostle. There are some situations in which my husband is a disciple and I'm the apostle, and vice versa.

Thinking about your own journey to motherhood and your current situation, would you describe yourself as more of a disciple or an apostle? Are there certain areas or issues you have mastered? Are there other issues that continue to challenge you? Write about these areas and identify your level of discovery (disciple or apostle) on the lines provided:

____

____

Perhaps the most beautiful part about networking with other moms is finding out we are all apostles and disciples of something. When my children start to date I will quickly become a disciple, and I will seek out other apostles who have "been there and done that."

How are we to interact with each other according to Colossians 3:16?

____

____

What experiences could you share with others in order to teach and admonish them? Instead of spouting out phrases starting with the dreaded words, "You really should," I pray our words will come from a place of love, concern, and genuine empathy. Some suggestions for how to share your experiences might include, "One thing that worked for us . . ." or "I'm so sorry. How can I help?" When we allow others to share without judging them, we help our network grow stronger, and our communication becomes clearer.

> *"Let the peace of Christ rule in your hearts, since as members of one body you were called to peace. And be thankful."*
> *—Colossians 3:15*

Colossians 3:15 says we are members of one body, and I can't think of a better body to be a part of than the many moms God has placed in my life. Jesus chose twelve men to be with him all the time, in every situation. These apostles shared in the vision Jesus had for bringing God's love into the world. Jesus knew it would be necessary to partner with these men in order to carry out God's will. By equipping them, Jesus was able to trust them to shape the future of the church and continue the ministry he started. As I continue on my journey, I understand how the women in my network have helped equip me for the various roles I play.

None of us are "just" a mother. We're so much more, and we need more than just one type of friend in our lives. Picture yourself standing among all the women in the world. Everyone has been gathered together, and suddenly you hear Christ call out your name. As you step forward, you hear him also call out the names of the women in your current mothers' group or Bible study. Standing in a circle, you look around at the faces in your group and you begin to smile. You realize, through God's perfect wisdom, that he's chosen different personalities and backgrounds and joined them in a common bond. Like the disciples, your group has been brought together and is being sent out to change the world. The great part about this scenario is that it isn't something we have to imagine—it can be our reality!

Take a moment to think about the important people in your life. Record their names and roles in your life. One friend might make you laugh while another one is brutally honest. Our desire is to record the positive, healthy attributes our friends and family bring into our lives. Feel free to add more connections if needed.

Look at this beautiful network God has placed around you. You're all connected and they need you just as much as you need them!

As Christian women, we are called to be disciples of Christ and apostles to this world, while also fulfilling our role of "mother."
#MomEssentials

Some of you might be thinking, "I don't need anyone else. I'm doing just fine on my own. I don't have time for other women in my life right now." If these statements are in your heart and mind, let me caution you against listening to them. You don't have to prove you can conquer this season alone. Having a community of women around you is not only healthy; it is necessary. Your personal well-being is not the only thing at stake.

I believe God cares so much about us that he not only meets our needs but also looks beyond them to equip us for our calling. Our calling is important because we are in the process of raising the next generation. Our children will become the citizens that shape the future. We must be ready to accept the fact that their impact on the world can be a beautiful extension of our parenting. As Christian women, we are called to be disciples of Christ and apostles to this world, while also fulfilling our role of "mother." These titles might seem intimidating, but they are attainable if we connect with one another and support each other every step of the way.

The women within your network are vital parts of God's plan to help you be put together, shaped up, and equipped. When we acknowledge God's perfect design, we begin to see the people around us as tools in the Master's hands. The women surrounding you are beautiful gifts. It's up to you to accept them. It can be awkward at first, especially if there's an age difference, but I challenge you to discover the stories and experiences they can share. Along with accepting these gifts of growth, you can help other moms be better equipped by sharing your own insights and discoveries.

Look at our Mom Moment for this chapter from Romans 12:10 and respond to the questions below.

1. How do you show you are devoted to the women in your network?

____

____

____

2. How do you show love to the women in your life?

____

____

____

3. What does a devoted community look like, sound like, and act like?

____

____

____

Satan would love nothing more than to disturb our community with gossip, grudges, or backbiting. In order to fight against Satan's attacks, we need to put on the full armor of God (**Ephesians 6:10-18**) and apply our knowledge of Scripture. Satan will try to undermine the importance of meeting together—I challenge you to silence his lies! Real friends and the mothers you've networked with don't care if you are wearing makeup or if you are a bit late. The important thing to do is to keep meeting together and keep encouraging each other (**Hebrews 10:25**). I challenge you to ignore the temptation to think you are alone. Speak up, share often, and enjoy the fact that you will sometimes be someone's disciple and other times you will be the apostle. Enjoy each opportunity to share your story and learn from others. God will equip you with what you need to be successful in your learning and teaching. He's called you to this place of discovery and application, and he has so much in store for you!

It can be difficult to relate to other moms, but they need you and you need them. When you feel as though your contribution to the world is small, remember that you're a member of an amazing team. We're team "mom" and we need to love, support, and encourage each other every day. When you're feeling down, find another mom, even a complete stranger, and give her a compliment. You'll see her countenance change

NOTES

and her eyes light up as you acknowledge her efforts. Connecting with other moms and showing them love helps us remember God's love for us. You are changing the world, one diaper at a time. You are shaping the future with each homework assignment and school project your kids complete. If your children are grown, you have the opportunity to influence and encourage others with your perspective and experience. Each of you is important to God's plan for this world, and I'm thankful for your commitment to the Word of God and to your family.

I love the promise found in verse 11 from our scripture in Ecclesiastes. Discover the promise of God's faithfulness from Ecclesiastes 3:11:

"He has made ________________
________________ in its
________________."

God is making something beautiful out of your network of friends and family. His timing is perfect and your effort is the reason this network continues to grow and become stronger. God is making something beautiful through you and your group. When we are devoted to each other, we see God's love and his plan in action.

CLOSING PRAYER

Lord, help me extend love to the women around me and accept their love in my life. Sometimes I feel like I'm the only one struggling, because everyone else looks so put together, rested, and relaxed. Help me to learn from these women and not see their exterior characteristics as a threat. Lord, I want to be your disciple and an apostle to this world. I know you have a beautiful purpose for my life. Help me hear your voice and learn from the network of women around me so I can go forward with confidence. I know you are equipping me to carry out the calling you've placed on my life. Thank you for devoting so much love and time to me and for helping me devote my life to my friends and family. I love you, Lord. Amen.

10

THE NEXT STEP

Mom Essential: SURRENDER

MOM MOMENT

Romans 12:1:
"Therefore, I urge you, brothers and sisters, in view of God's mercy, to offer your bodies as a living sacrifice, holy and pleasing to God—this is your true and proper worship."

One of my favorite worship choruses contains the line "I surrender all." I sing those words and pray that I'd truly be able to give God everything. Unfortunately, surrender hasn't been a one-time event for me. I have to make a daily choice to surrender everything to God and let go.

We've tackled some pretty personal and sometimes touchy subject areas over the course of this study. Each of us has begun a journey that will continue until we take our last breath here on earth. Reading about God's promises and applying them to our lives is important, but it isn't easy. One of my favorite verses comes from Philippians 1:6:

> "Being confident of this, that he who began
> a __________ __________ in you will
> ______________ it on to completion until
> the day of Christ Jesus."

For surrender to be possible, I first have to trust. Trusting God requires me to have confidence that he is in control and that he has a plan. Once I establish my confidence in God's ability, I interpret the events in my life as part of the "good work" God is doing to help me become the mother and woman he wants me to be.

God is working on our behalf beyond our earthly roles. Being a mom is a major part of the work God is perfecting in our lives. As we come to the end of our study, let's review the ten essentials and what we took away from each chapter. Surrender isn't something that happens one time or in one area of our lives. As we review each chapter's essential, take a moment to write out the Mom Moment scripture and what you took away or remember most.

CHAPTER/ ESSENTIAL	MOM MOMENT	MY TAKE-AWAY
1—Balance	Hebrews 4:12	
2—Strength	Psalm 105:4	
3—Honesty	Matthew 6:20-21	
4—Identity	Matthew 5:13-14	
5—Growth	Isaiah 43:19*a*	
6—Perspective	Matthew 19:26	
7—Discipline	Ecclesiastes 3:1	
8—Preparation	Galatians 6:7*b*	
9—Networking	Romans 12:10*a*	
10—Surrender	Romans 12:1	

I hope you have time to reflect, pray, and listen to God as you review each essential. Let's continue the good work God has begun in our lives. Listen to the Holy Spirit's guidance and respond in truth as you continue applying these essentials to your life.

By bringing a unity and connection to the essentials we've studied, we see how equipped we are to face anything that comes our way. Each of us signed our name to a commitment to study Scripture and have an active prayer life. I hope each of us will continue to make that commitment a reality in our daily life. We don't know what tomorrow will bring, but we know God is in control.

From the beginning of time, God has been putting things together. He created the heavens and the earth. The first chapter of Genesis tells us that the earth was formless, empty, and dark. I've stood in a cave, hundreds of feet below the earth's surface, and experienced complete darkness. It is almost suffocating how hopeless and vast darkness can seem. But when God puts things together, he brings light. Record what God put together in **Psalm 139:13-14**:

> "For you created my inmost being; you __________ _______
>
> __________________ in my mother's womb. I praise you because
>
> _____ am fearfully and wonderfully made; your works are
>
> ___________________, I know that full well."

God creates wonderful things, and you and I are products of his creativity. We can trust God's desire to connect with us and provide for us.

God created our world so light and life would thrive. Even when Adam and Eve disobeyed God by listening to Satan's lies, God didn't leave them in a place of darkness and despair. There were consequences, but God had a plan. God wanted a relationship with his creation, but sin had forever disfigured the beautiful connection between God and man. Jesus' birth, death, and resurrection allowed God to restore the lines of communication with us and offer us salvation. **First Peter 1:3** explains this beautiful gift from God, through his Son, Jesus.

"Praise be to the ________ and ______________ of our Lord Jesus Christ! In his great mercy he has given us ___________ ______________ into a living hope through the resurrection of Jesus Christ from the dead."

Through Jesus' resurrection, we can approach the throne of God with confidence and trust that when we admit our sins, God is faithful and will forgive us. (See **1 John 1:9**.) While the forgiveness of sins and the thought of eternal life with God are wonderful promises, they can seem a bit philosophical and not very practical to our everyday life. But because God put this plan together, he sent Jesus to come and broaden our understanding of him.

Jesus' disciples were concerned because they heard Jesus talking about leaving them. In their humanity, they wondered how Jesus could leave without setting up a kingdom on earth. Jesus' ministry on earth lasted for about three years. Within that time, he did everything he could to prepare his followers for his impending crucifixion. Jesus wanted them to understand that evil wouldn't win but his death was necessary in order for mankind to have life.

Take a moment to read the entire chapter of **John 14**. When I read this portion of Scripture, I can almost sense Jesus' tone. He sounds a bit frustrated with his disciples. I imagine Jesus had shared these same words and concepts with them many times before. Countless times, I've told something to my children, yet I find I still have to repeat myself. After reading chapter 14, fill in the missing words from verses 25-27.

"All this I have spoken while still with you. But the Advocate, the __________ ____________, whom the Father will send in my name, will _____________ you all things and will remind you of _________________ I have said to you. _____________ I leave with you; my peace I give you. I do not give to you as the world gives. Do not let your _____________ be troubled and do not be afraid."

I love how tender and compassionate Jesus was with his disciples, even while being a bit frustrated at their lack of understanding. Jesus assured them that they wouldn't be left alone. He had to leave so the Spirit could come. Through the Holy Spirit we find ourselves equipped to handle life because our Advocate, our helper, reminds us of God's promises and continues to teach us. What a wonderful gift! *The Message* translates these same verses into today's verbiage:

> I'm telling you these things while I'm still living with you. The Friend, the Holy Spirit whom the Father will send at my request, will make everything plain to you. He will remind you of all the things I have told you. I'm leaving you well and whole. That's my parting gift to you. Peace. I don't leave you the way you're used to being left—feeling abandoned, bereft. So don't be upset. Don't be distraught. (John 14:25-27, TM)

Sweet sisters in Christ, we have a friend in God, in Jesus, and in the Holy Spirit. They work together to help us be put together, shaped up, and equipped to do the work we've been called to complete here on earth. Heaven is watching. Heaven is cheering us on—we aren't alone!

Using our previous chart as a reference, we can see the connection between our three themes (put together, shaped up, and equipped), ten essentials, and the Holy Trinity (God, Jesus, and the Holy Spirit). Each of these areas works together to help the essentials we've studied become a reality in our lives. In each circle, the chapters are labeled. As you fill in the essential for each chapter, I pray you'll begin to see the connection between each essential and the theme it falls under. The shaded areas are provided for you to record any essential you are struggling to master right now in your life. After recording which essentials you need the most help to accomplish, surrender those to God. He created you and he can handle any struggles you bring him. I hope it becomes clear that we can trust God's ability to put us together, Jesus' sacrificial love that shapes us into who we are becoming, and the Holy Spirit's constant presence that will equip us to continue our growth.

Notice the word in the middle of our chart: balance. No one can successfully walk the tightrope of life without some help. Our lives will remain balanced when we trust that God, Jesus, and the Holy Spirit are working on our behalf and will never let us fall. Believing this statement takes a lot of faith. Our faith grows stronger as we apply these essentials to our lives. When we actively focus on the essentials, the "extras" of this world won't gain a stronghold in our lives. Our spirit will be filled with

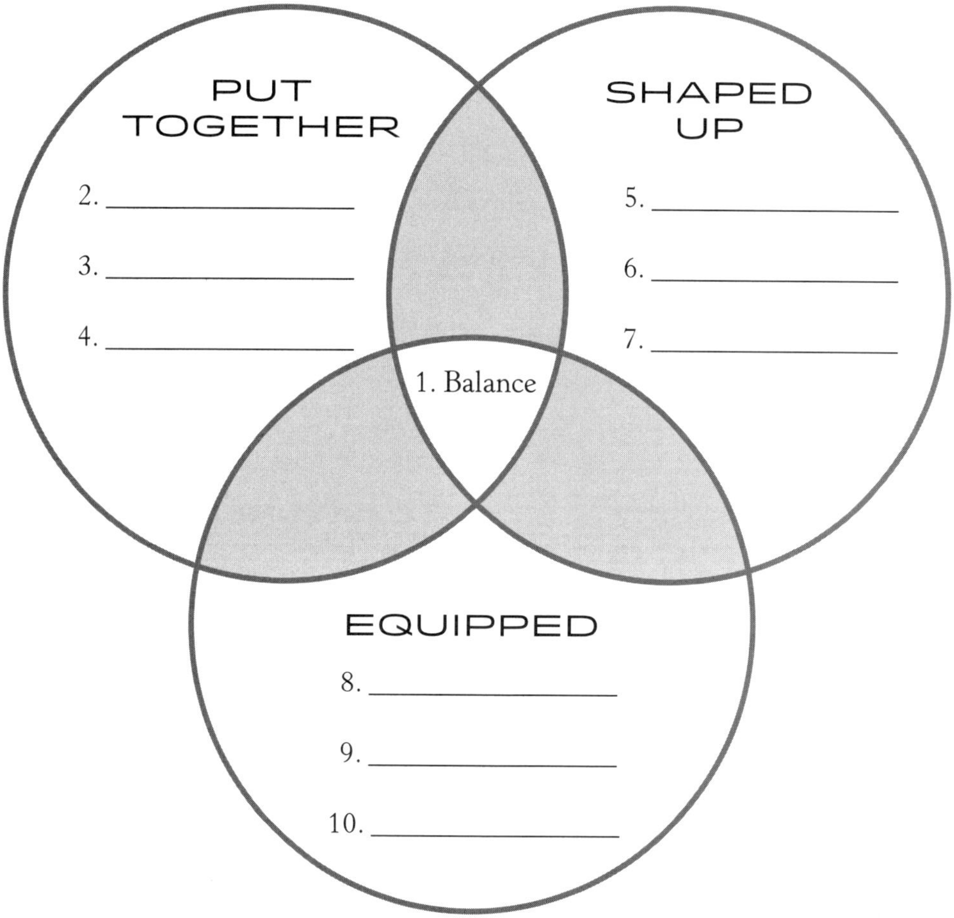

the promises from Scripture, and there won't be room for fear or anxiety to abide. We have to be vigilant—we can't give up! In **John 16:33,** Jesus made a declaration that brings us hope when we feel tempted to give up on ourselves or our situation.

> "I have told you these things, so that in me you may have ____________. In this world you will have ____________. But take heart! I have ____________ the world."

Trouble is going to come, but when my life is surrendered to God's plan, I can experience the peace he promises to provide. The love of Christ has conquered the world, and it can conquer my fears too. We can take heart and take action. By applying these ten essentials to our lives and claiming the promises we've discovered in Scripture, we can be more than conquerors! Discover this truth from **Romans 8:38-39** and speak it out loud as a declaration for your life. You are living according to the essentials, not the extras, and *nothing* will throw us off balance when we're focused on the promises of Scripture.

"For I am convinced that neither ____________ nor __________,

neither angels nor demons, neither the ________________

nor the _______________, nor any powers, neither height nor

depth, nor _________________ else in all creation, will be able to

__________________ us from the love of _________ that is in

Christ Jesus our Lord."

Nothing can separate us from God's love. We can surrender our lives with complete confidence in God's desire to love us and carry us through this life. You and I have been chosen, and we have the love of Christ to guide us. I pray we continue to choose the promises of Scripture over the chaos of this world. Thank you for being committed to this time of growth and discovery. I can't *wait* to see what God has in store for all of us in the days ahead!

CLOSING PRAYER

Use the space provided to write your own prayer to God. Call out to him. Praise him. Share your heart. He is listening and waiting. Your prayers are like sweet incense to our heavenly Father. The One who has put you together, shaped you, and is equipping you will not leave you. He's in each moment of your day, and he can't wait to hear your heart.

NOTES

CHAPTER 1

1. Oswald Chambers, *My Utmost for His Highest: An Updated Edition in Today's Language* (Grand Rapids, MI: Discovery House Publishers, 1992), August 28.

CHAPTER 4

1. Chambers, *My Utmost for His Highest,* July 15.
2. Ibid.

CHAPTER 5

1. Matthew Henry, "Mark 7." *Matthew Henry's Commentary on the Whole Bible.* BibleStudyTools.com. http://www.biblestudytools.com/commentaries/matthew-henry-complete/mark/7.html?p=7 (Accessed February 11, 2014).
2. Ibid.
3. Ibid.

CHAPTER 9

1. John MacArthur, *Twelve Ordinary Men* (Nashville: Thomas Nelson, 2002), xv.